Sharing
Sacred
Stories

Sharing Sacred Stories

Current Approaches to Spiritual
Direction and Guidance

ROBERT FRAGER
Editor

A Crossroad Book
The Crossroad Publishing Company
New York

The Crossroad Publishing Company
16 Penn Plaza, Suite 1550, New York, NY 10001

Printed in the United States of America

Library of Congress Cataloging-in-Publication Data

Sharing sacred stories: contemporary approaches to spiritual direction and guidance / edited by Robert Frager.
   p.cm.
 ISBN-13: 978-0-8245-2446-3 (alk. paper)
 ISBN-10: 0-8245-2446-2 (alk. paper)
 1. Spirituality. 2. Spiritual direction. 3. Transpersonal psychology.
 I. Frager, Robert, 1940- II. Title.

 BL624.S483 2007
 206'.1–dc22
 2007002711

1 2 3 4 5 6 7 8 9 10   12 11 10 09 08 07

Contents

ALTERNATIVE SETTINGS FOR SPIRITUAL DIRECTION

GROUP SPIRITUAL DIRECTION

Sharing Sacred Stories

In this book we seek to explore new developments in spiritual guidance and, in particular, to examine the interface of spiritual guidance and transpersonal psychology. Many of these essayists are both psychologists and spiritual guides, and they offer insights from both fields. They demonstrate the practical and theoretical value of transpersonal psychology for spiritual guidance.

Transpersonal psychology is committed to the study of the full range of human experience, from psychotic and maladaptive behavior to the heights of inspired and mystical experiences. The field recognizes the value of spirituality as a powerful dimension of human experience. Carl Jung first coined the term transpersonal (*uberpersonlich*) when he used the phrase "transpersonal unconscious" as a synonym for "collective unconscious."

Unfortunately, spirituality has long been regarded as off-limits in other fields of psychology. Too often psychologists have regarded spirituality as a private matter not to be included in research or in clinical work. Traditional psychology has seriously underestimated the potent influence of spirituality in the lives of most people. Spiritual guidance can benefit from the insights and knowledge of psychology. However, it cannot work with a psychology that ignores or even pathologizes spirituality. Spiritual guidance and transpersonal psychology complement each other.

A key stimulus for the establishment of transpersonal psychology was Abraham Maslow's research on self-actualizing persons. Maslow's work included the study of peak experiences, inspired creativity, higher ideals, and altruistic service beyond personal concerns and

1

motivations. Maslow argued that spirituality is essential to our health and well being. "Without the transcendent and the transpersonal, we get sick, violent and nihilistic, or else hopeless and apathetic."[1] From a transpersonal point of view, spiritual guidance provides nourishment for the soul, essential nourishment for every human being.

Transpersonal psychology is complex and multi-dimensional. The following points[2] provide a sense of its varied elements:

1. Transpersonal psychology is a psychology of health and human potential. While transpersonal psychology does recognize and address human psychopathology, it does not base its model of the human psyche from the ill or diseased. Transpersonal psychology looks to saints, prophets, artists, heroes, and heroines for models of full human development and of the growth-oriented nature of the normal human psyche. Instead of defining ourselves as all essentially neurotic (if not worse), transpersonal psychology holds the individual as one engaged in the process of development toward full humanity, as exemplified by the lives of great men and women.

2. Rather than being a recent innovation, transpersonal psychology is largely a return to the perennial philosophy identified by Aldous Huxley. Mystical experience, spiritual disciplines, and shamanistic healing practices, which have been central concerns of humankind for millennia, are also a focus of transpersonal psychology.

3. Transpersonal psychology is depth psychology. It is part of the therapeutic stream started by Freud and his successors, Jung, Rank, and Reich. Roberto Assagioli, who posited a superconscious, as well as a subconscious, integrated transpersonal and depth psychology, as did Carl Jung.

4. Transpersonal psychology does not see the human personality as an end in itself. Our personal history and our resulting personality traits and tendencies are seen as the coating covering

our transpersonal essence. Another way of putting this is that the personality is, by design, the vessel or vehicle that enables the soul and spirit to navigate through the world. Thus, the proper role of the personality is to be a translucent window, a servant to divinity within. The "trans" in transpersonal has two senses—to rise above as in transcendent and to pass through as in transparent.

5. Transpersonal psychology is a psychology of human development. As developmental psychologists, we recognize there is a continuum of development. This continuum begins with individuals who have not achieved a stable personality and strong ego identity, people who might be called psychotic. Up the next step of the developmental ladder are those with "borderline personality disorder," in whom an unstable sense of self and partially integrated personality have developed. Another step toward full functionality are those with a strong sense of ego identity and functioning personality, the so-called "normals." Transpersonal psychology, at this point, extends beyond traditional psychology by addressing later stages of human development, in which there is disidentification from one's personality or personal identity. The next stage is typified by the states of consciousness obtained by advanced meditators and mystics. A final step in development is posited in which the person realizes a state of unity (i.e., oneness with God or enlightenment), a state seen in the greatest saints and mystics.

6. Transpersonal psychology is an approach to the whole person. It seeks a balanced development of the intellectual, emotional, spiritual, physical, social, and creative expression aspects of a person's life. Thus, all six areas are addressed scholastically and therapeutically, and integration or balance is sought. This is the educational model developed at the Institute of Transpersonal Psychology, the leading educational institution in transpersonal psychology.

7. Transpersonal psychology is a psychology that goes through the personal to the transpersonal. Far from simply transcending our humanity, it is a process of working *through* our humanity, in an inclusive way, to reach the recognition of divinity within. In this sense, transpersonal psychology emerges out of personal psychology, as a result of the individual's growth and maturation.

8. Transpersonal psychology is the psychology of the twenty-first century. It is the future norm in psychology, as yet unrecognized by the mainstream. Transpersonal psychology builds on the psychoanalytic, behavioral/experimental, and humanistic psychologies that preceded it. It provides both an extension of and a different perspective from these previous psychologies. It is in no way a denial of the validity of their theories and techniques. It simply places them in a new context. Transpersonal psychology asserts that religious and mystical experiences and the perspectives that derive from them are valid approaches to reality and can be studied scientifically. It is the beginning attempt of science to understand these most meaningful of human experiences.

9. Transpersonal psychology recognizes and studies the different states and stations of consciousness. It recognizes that such different states as dreaming, hypnotic trance, prayer, and "waking" consciousness all have sub-levels within themselves and possess their own state-specific systems, their own realities. Further, transpersonal psychology recognizes that not only are there different states of consciousness that one may move into and out of during the course of a day but that there are also stages or stations of consciousness that, through development, one can come to live in relatively permanently.

10. The simplest definition is that transpersonal psychology is spiritual psychology. It recognizes that humanity has drives toward sex and aggression and also drives toward wholeness, toward connecting with and experiencing the divine.

There are four basic premises underlying transpersonal psychology:[3]

1. A transcendent reality or unity binds together all (apparently separate) phenomena.

2. The ego or individual self is but a reflection of a greater, transpersonal self (or Self). We come from and are grounded in that self. However, we have become estranged from our origins and we need to return to them in order to become fully healthy and whole human beings.

3. The fact that individuals can directly experience this reality or greater self is at the core of the spiritual dimensions of life.

4. This experience involves a qualitative shift in experiencing oneself and the larger world. It is a powerful, self-validating experience.

I hope that the insights and wisdom generously shared in these essays will touch your heart and stimulate your mind. May this book support continued dialog among spiritual guides, psychologists, and all those who have been called to the blessed work of tending the holy in ourselves and in others.

References

Maslow, Abraham. *Toward a Psychology of Being*. New York: Van Nostrand, 1968.

Valle, Ron. "The Emergence of Transpersonal Psychology." In *Existential-Phenomenological Perspectives in Psychology*, edited by R. Valle and S. Haling. New York: Plenum Press, 1989.

PERSPECTIVES ON SPIRITUAL DIRECTION AND GUIDANCE

The first section of this book provides perspectives on spirituality and spiritual guidance from differing religious and psychological traditions. The authors remind us of the breadth and depth of the work of spiritual guidance, and that this work has its roots in all of the world's wisdom traditions.

The first essay is by Huston Smith, one of the world's great teachers of comparative religion. Huston has truly made himself at home in each of the great faith traditions and has explored the deep truths within each. He truly exemplifies the extraordinary openness and wisdom of a great sage. Huston eloquently reflects on his own spiritual path and the many lessons he has learned. He reminds us that there are many spiritual paths, and different paths may be suitable for different people, because we all have diverse capacities and temperaments. Huston retells Plato's story of the cave and reminds us of Plato's conclusion, "Would not the one who has seen reality instead of shadow-play realize that the object of teaching is not to communicate facts, but rather first to see and then to help others to see?"

Jeremy Taylor brings to spiritual guidance the religious perspective of a Universalist Unitarian minister, the insights of a Jungian-oriented therapist, and the social commitment of a community organizer. He brings great passion and sophistication to working with our dreams as an effective method of deep self-understanding. Jeremy views working with dreams as an essential component in spiritual guidance. He has worked for over forty years with over thirteen thousand of his own dreams and with over one hundred thousand dreams of others. Jeremy illustrates how our dreams can bring us essential insights for our personal and spiritual journeys. One of his basic principles in working with dreams is that *all* dreams come in the service of health and wholeness and speak a universal language, even our nightmares.

Rabbi Zalman Schachter-Shalomi, another wise and venerable sage, raises four fundamental questions. "What ideas of cosmology do we need in order to approach the healing of the planet?"; "What is the basic health ethos arising from that new cosmology?"; "What are the practices and methods, the skillful means, needed to lift cultural trance and launch the awareness of the emerging cosmology?"; and "What adjustments in the social sciences, biology, physics, medicine, the arts, communications, philosophy, spiritual technologies, theology, and especially ethics do we need in order to heal the planet?" In effect Zalman is asking how we can develop a curriculum for saints and bodhisattvas.

Robert Frager outlines basic principles of spiritual psychology found in the Sufi mystical tradition. He discusses the transformation of the self or ego through seven stages, from the narcissistic and unconscious lower self to the state of unity found at the highest level of the pure self. Robert also discusses the four levels of the spiritual heart, and the Sufi approach of finding God within the depths of the heart. The breast is the outmost layer of the heart. At this level we interact with the world and struggle with the demands of the ego and the challenges of daily life. The heart proper is the level of inner knowledge. The intelligence of the heart is our spiritual intelligence. The inner heart is the level of spiritual vision and direct mystical experience. The innermost heart is beyond words and images. It is the temple of God within, created by God to house God's presence in us.

Reflections on the Spiritual Path

I have been around since transpersonal psychology was just beginning. I worked alongside Anthony Sutich and Abe Maslow, and so I feel I can discuss the field with some authority. As far as I am concerned, psychology today outside of ITP is mundane. It is all on a beginning level. There is nothing in it, even existentialism (although it did take a step forward with Rollo May, another good friend of mine), but existential psychology is still stuck on the ground floor of the universe. As Peter Berger has said, "If *anything* characterizes modernity, it's the loss of the sense of transcendence." He defines transcendence as: "a reality that encompasses and surpasses our everyday affairs." In the field of psychology, transpersonal has taken the lead toward achieving that transcendence and the impact has been far reaching.

One of the reasons the field has the ability to do this can be found in its name. "Transpersonal" is a wonderful word—it implies a greater perspective. Now what about psychology? I am not a psychologist, but I am, as Confucius said he was, a lover of the ancients. One of the reasons I love premodern views is they do not chop up the fabric of knowledge, which is seamless, into little pieces. In modernity, psychology goes one place, philosophy another. But consider Plato – was he a philosopher? Of course! Was he a theologian? Yes, if we study his allegory of the cave and what is outside. Was he a historian? He knew a lot of history and wrote about it. The ancients didn't snip up knowledge into little segments. My concern about psychology in general is that it picks up only a piece of this now shredded fabric of knowledge. However, there is the other side of psychology, transpersonal, which has a more inclusive viewpoint. Because transpersonal psychologists add on a spiritual awareness, they avoid the narrowing trap others fall into. What this means, though, is that transpersonal psychologists are also a form of spiritual guide. This is a great responsibility, and can be a confusing and difficult way to practice.

What I will do here is touch on a number of points that have some bearing on spiritual guidance. My hope is that readers will pick up some nuggets that are useful to their work in the transpersonal field.

One of the benefits of being a veteran teacher for fifty years is that along the way certain students connect with what you are saying, and they become your friends. One student of mine like that is Neal Grossman. Neal has children and grandchildren in Berkeley so he comes twice a year to visit his family, and he always comes by and spends a morning with me. During our last visit he said, "Huston, there is something that is very important to me, and I've never told you about it. I wanted you to know."

I leaned forward in my chair, and he told me his story: "I was a senior in high school. I liked science, I liked literature, I liked classical music. One Saturday afternoon, with nothing much to do, I decided to go across the Charles River to Boston. Wandering around aimlessly, I found myself passing an imposing building: the Boston Public Library. I felt a desire to go in, and so I did. The first thing that amazed me was how many books there are in the world. Walking down one of the aisles, my eye fell upon a thick volume: *The Dialogues* of Plato. I had heard of Plato, but I had never read him. So I seized the book and went to a reading table. I let that thick book fall open and it opened to the beginning of the seventh book of *The Republic,* which is where Plato tells his 'Allegory of the Cave.'"

It is important to remember this allegory before finishing Neal's story.

In the beginning of the seventh book, Plato issues an invitation. He says (in my paraphrase), come with me, if you will, and try to visualize a cave with a row of prisoners chained in such a way that they can only see the back wall of the cave. At the back of them is a bonfire, and between the bonfire and these prisoners is a ceaseless procession of puppeteers parading all the things you can think of: tables, chairs, cabbages and kings, and their likes. All the prisoners can see is two-dimensional black cut-out objects. Plato continues again with another invitation: Come with me, if you will, another step. Let us imagine that one of these prisoners is released. He turns around, and the first thing he sees is fire, the bonfire and color. That's staggering enough, but then behind it he sees the opening of the cave. He goes toward it, and when he steps out he finds himself in an utterly incredible universe. This world is technicolor, not black and white. It is three-dimensional, and above it all, the sun shines its rays down on all the beauty. When the released prisoner returns to those who are still chained and tells them that what they are looking at is not the real world, they probably think he is off his rocker. However, Plato closes his allegory by saying, would not the man who had seen the great out-of-doors realize that the object of teaching is not to communicate facts, but rather first to see and then to help others to see?

I come now to why Neal told me this story. "When I came to the end of those two pages," he said, "I found that there were tears streaming down my cheeks."

A natural question might be "What caused those tears?"

I will venture an answer. There is within us – in even the blithest, most lighthearted among us – a fundamental dis-ease. It acts like an unquenchable fire that renders the vast majority of us incapable in this life of ever coming to full peace. This desire lies in the marrow of our bones and the deep regions of our souls. All great literature, poetry, art, philosophy, psychology, and religion tries to name and analyze this longing. We are seldom in direct touch with it, and indeed the modern world seems set on preventing us from *getting* in touch with it by covering it with an unending phantasmagoria of entertainments, obsessions, addictions, and distractions of every sort. But the longing is there, built into us like a jack-in-the-box that presses for release. Whether we realize it or not, simply to be human is to long for release from mundane existence, with its confining walls of finitude and mortality. Neal, as a young man, came into contact with something that released him, helped him to see, and that is why he cried.

Remember Carl Jung, who said so many significant things, one of which was that it is only the things we do not understand that have any meaning. I find this very arresting. We do not understand this deepest element within us that is seeking release, and it plays a tremendous part in directing our lives. As spiritual guides, transpersonal psychologists must be attuned to this deepest element in themselves, their students, their teachers, and their clients.

I have been very fortunate in having had a number of famous friends. Aldous Huxley was my guru for about fifteen years. I brought him to MIT for a semester as Distinguished Professor of Humanities. He said something in his seminar I will never forget. "The problem that life poses for us is to do our best to overcome the fundamental disability of being human: egocentrism, putting ourselves before other people." I think that sets the direction for our stress. We can't get rid of it totally but we can try to reduce it. Ego strength is good, but egocentricity is bad. What can we do to reduce that disability within us? How can we find the spiritual release we seek?

Mentioning Aldous Huxley raises the question of the role of the guru or teacher in the spiritual quest. We all know that we live in a time of fallen gurus, but we ought not to let that jeopardize the role of an authentic guru in the spiritual quest. In our younger days, our parents are role models. They are our gurus. We wouldn't know how to shape our lives except in terms of their example. In college, one of my professors became in effect my guru. My life was unformed, and he gave me a mold for me to pour my life into-teaching- and in all of the eight great religions that I have given my career to studying I have had a guru. If you ever pass by my house in Berkeley, ring the bell, and I will show you the photographs on the wall of my study honoring my gurus and inspiring me to live the way those people lived. My Native American guru, Reuben Snake, is among them. When I was first introduced to him, he held out his hand and said, "I'm Reuben Snake, your humble serpent." (Humor wasn't his only virtue.) We all need many different guides.

One of the people I have been blessed by coming close to is His Holiness the Dalai Lama. For thirty-five years he has befriended me. I recently heard that when someone asked him how things were going, he sighed and said, "My responsibilities to my people are so heavy that I can only meditate two hours a day. Before I drop the body, I would like to become enlightened, but there is no way I can become enlightened by meditating only two hours a day." Then my informant said he heard him sigh and say softly, as if to himself, "Well, maybe enlightenment isn't very important after all."

We can all hear the ring of authenticity in that statement, and it can puncture our balloons, if we have the inflated idea that the point of spiritual guidance is to enable our clients to become enlightened. We have to tone it down a little bit. Hopefully we can help them to progress toward enlightenment, and that will be a great service if we can effect it.

Jung, Huxley, and the Dalai Lama provide some examples of spiritual guidance in my own practice, but I also have another tool. I have found the Hindu doctrine of the four yogas to be important. People have different temperaments. Some are reflective and follow Jnana yoga, the way to God through knowledge; some are affective, given to love, or Bhakti yoga. Some people are drawn to service, Karma yoga, and some to meditation, Raja yoga.

The Hindu doctrine states that we all have all four of these capabilities within us, but it is like a hand of cards, in different proportions. It behooves us to lead with our strong suit for we get more spiritual mileage out of what we are good at. Kendra, my wife, is a meditator. Her practice is Vipassana meditation. She can go deep very fast. I put in thirty years paying my dues to meditation, which climaxed in a summer in a Zen monastery doing nothing for ten weeks but meditating. What did I learn?

I learned I was not a Raja yogi. I am a meditation washout. I am a Jnana yogi. For me, the way to God is through knowledge, but this knowledge has nothing to do with encyclopedic knowledge of facts and logical dexterity. It is more like seeing, the feeling Neal had when he read Plato. When I am sitting at my computer and working on a frontier problem—one that is at the growing tip of the understanding that I am trying to give birth to-I can often feel it coming. And then I look out of that window at the sky, and it kicks in. I feel exalted. When I go back to the computer: *Yes!* I can say it a little better now.

As studying the four yogas showed me, a profound teacher and partner in the journey toward peace is that deepest element of the self, the part constantly seeking release that I mentioned earlier. We can all be guided spiritually by our unconscious selves. I have an example of this process from my own life. A few years back, the *LA Times* religion reporter called and she said, "We want to do a profile on you. If I fly up, can you give me an afternoon?"

I said, "Yes, gladly."

So in the course of wandering over innumerable questions, she asked, "Do you have any spiritual practices?"

I said, "Yes, from as early as I can remember I have three: body, mind, and soul. First, body. I begin with about ten to fifteen minutes of Hatha yoga. For thirty-five years my favorite asana pose was standing on my head. I love that pose, but five years ago osteoporosis hit me, a fracture in the back. I've phased from Hatha yoga into physical therapy. Same thing, different word.

"Next the mind. I'm not the first one to set out on a spiritual quest. Others have done it, and they've done it better than I'm doing it. So for the mind, I read two or three pages of one of the sacred texts. It can be the Bible; it can be the Tao Te Ching; it can be the Bhagavad Gita, whatever. And then something for the spirit follows that. For me it's a pendulum swing between prayer and meditation, and no sharp line between the two. Usually prayer is verbal, and meditation is not, but there are levels in prayer and the highest level is the prayer of silence. There you have my spiritual practices."

I was sitting back to wait for the reporter's next question, but then something kicked in, and I said, "Well, you know, there is one more. For the last fifteen years, I've added another spiritual practice."

She said, "What's that?"

I said, "Composting."

She wrote that down, and when that profile hit the press, that was the first line in her profile: "Huston Smith Composts as a Spiritual Practice." Although it sounds amusing, composting is just as important for me as the other three. It grounds me. I got into composting when a six-year-old granddaughter spent a week with us. Some six-year-olds are happy to sit with the television. This one was a self-starter and needed projects. We got into composting, and she was fascinated by my description of turning it over, aerating it. At the end, our compost came out so good it needed a name. She suggested Perfect Dirt. The week ended with her out on the sidewalk with a big sign that said "Free Perfect Dirt," and she handed out plastic bags of the stuff. She went on to better things, and eventually she became a science writer in marine biology, but I have never given up making perfect dirt. Of course we have an ecological crisis, and you can question what a few wheelbarrows of perfect dirt will do, but that attitude misses the point. The point is *what does it do for me?* And what it does is to move me into the ecological cycle. As a philosopher I live a lot in my head, and it does me good to get my hands dirty. But more important, composting phases me into the cycles of nature, all of which involve giving and getting. We take a lot from the earth, and it fulfills me to give something back, even if it is only a token, in the way of good, restored soil. I had not planned on answering the reporter in that way, but my answer was deeply true.

Although sometimes wisdom comes easily, like it did in that interview, becoming a spiritual guide is not an effortless process of allowing your unconscious to do all the work. I know what I am talking about here, and I will spell out the evidence that shows that I know. I studied Zen Buddhism for a number of years. The roshi (Zen master) gives his students koans, which are very strange riddles. Two standard ones are: "What was your face before your parents were born?" and "What is the sound of one hand clapping?" I knocked my head out trying to solve these. I was given the mu koan, which is short for the face before your ancestors were born, and I had to go in twice a day to confront the roshi and give him my answers.

Every day when I went in and gave him my answer he would say, "No, no, no." Then he would ring his little bell and say, "Go back! Go back! Go back!" This went on for ten weeks. During the last week, we were subjected to a new technique: sleep deprivation. They let me off easy because I was older. Most of the students were in their early twenties, and I was thirty-seven so I was allowed three and a half hours of sleep.

After the first night of three and a half hours of sleep, I was tired. After the second night, I was more so, but there was no napping because we had a *jikki jitzu*, a sergeant at arms, to whack us if we showed any signs of drowsiness. When I went into the roshi on the afternoon of the sixth day of this eight-day intensive, I was out of my mind. I mean that literally. It is known that sleep deprivation drives you psychotic. You have to have those dreams.

I stormed into my roshi that afternoon, resolved not just to throw in the towel but to throw it right in his face. There is a ritual involved in the interviews. I sank to my knees, touched my forehead to the tatami mat, and then sat back on my haunches and locked eyes with the roshi. He looked like he was glaring at me, which he often did, and he said, "How is it going?"

I exploded, "*Terrible!*"

He said, "You think you're going to get sick, don't you?"

I yelled at him, "Yes I think I'm going to get sick!" My throat was beginning to close up, and I had to struggle for my breath.

Then the miracle happened.

His tone of voice changed, modulated, and his expression was not all taunting. He said, "What is sickness? What is health? Put them aside, and go forward." What I will always have difficulty expressing is how those simple words came through to me. I found myself saying to myself, "Well, by god, he's right!" I left the audience room, not only resolved to stick it out the next two days, but knowing that I could.

In summary, I have tried to articulate my conviction that, first, transpersonal psychology is an important supplement to other varieties because it gives greater recognition to the divine component within us that can inform us if we attend to it carefully; and second, because it underscores more heavily the need for a variety of spiritual guides. "The wind blows where it chooses, and you hear the sound of it; but you do not know where it comes from or where it goes. So it is with everyone who is born of the Spirit."[4] Which is to say, no spiritual guide can cathect with everyone who needs guidance.

Dreams and Spiritual Guidance

Before discussing the issue of dreams and spiritual guidance, I need to begin with a caveat. I am an itinerant preacher, and we are a notoriously untrustworthy breed. No one should take the word of an itinerant preacher for *anything*, let alone anything as potentially important as what the deeper meanings of your dreams might be. I am also in somewhat of an awkward position when considering dreams and spiritual guidance because I hold passionate beliefs about the topic. Dreams can play a very important role in energizing and guiding the course of spiritual development. I will not present these ideas in some quasi-academic, even-handed way. I'm going to share what I think and what I believe, and I specifically do not want my enthusiasm for the topic to be mistaken as a stealth request that anyone take my word for any of what I have to say.

Essentially, I would like to capitalize on the interest in dreams that I perceive in the room, and in the world today. Hopefully, at the end of this discussion I will have piqued that interest even further, not only in relation to your own dreams, but also and especially with regard to other peoples' dreams.

I have been doing this work now for about forty years (counting the apprenticeship time while I worked up nerve enough to charge money for it). I made a deal with myself forty years ago that I would record in my journal everything that I remembered from the dream world, no matter how "confused," or "trivial," or "distressing" it might seem at first glance, and I have maintained that commitment to myself for the past four decades. As Edith Piaf said, *"Je regret rien."* It has been, and continues to be, an immensely useful and rewarding practice, and — it marks me as a fanatic.

I do not believe that every one needs to record and journal about every remembered dream in order to get the immense benefit, spiritual and otherwise, that comes from dreaming, but my journal is my primary research tool. Recently, I recorded the 13,581st of my dreams, (which, if you divide it out by forty years, is really not that many. It only comes out to an average of slightly less than one dream a night). A conservative estimate is that I hear ten dreams from other people, in one way and another, for every one of my own dreams I am able to remember and record. This means I am drawing my conclusions about the fundamental nature of dreaming from a sample size significantly in excess of one hundred thousand dreams. Even though it is obviously a large enough sample to draw valid statistical inferences from, it is still a biased sample, and I need to acknowledge that to begin with. It is made up only of people who trusted me enough to tell me their dreams, or trusted the world enough to put their dreams out into some kind of public form, written or otherwise. It may, in fact, be the case that there are dreams, kinds of dreams, or classes of dreams that I have never heard of. I don't think so, but I have to acknowledge that possibility.

Out of all the dreams I have had or heard, the most important thing that I have come to believe is that *all dreams,* and I emphasize "all," *come in the service of health and wholeness and speak a universal language.*

Now obviously on the face of it, that does not appear to be true. My suspicion is that just about everybody has at some time or another had a dream or two that were so *nasty*, so noxious, that they didn't seem to have anything even remotely to do with health and wholeness. We usually call those dreams "nightmares."

What I would ask you to consider with regard to the nightmare form is the evidence of our evolutionary history. If you take the fossil record at all seriously, if you take the more recent DNA evidence at all seriously — all of which I do — there is compelling reason to believe that we human beings have been scratching and scrabbling around, attempting to survive and reproduce in a wide range of ecological circumstances, for something in the neighborhood of seven million years. One of the primary strategies, I would even argue *the* primary strategy that we have adopted as a species in order to stay alive and thrive is to cultivate our consciousness to the point where we are able to recognize threat at an early enough stage of its development that we can make educated guesses about its speed and direction, and get out of the way. Simple contemplation will demonstrate, I think, that those of us who are able to pull off this trick of consciousness are much more likely to survive over the longer haul than those of us who dither around and can't quite get it together to do that.

Since this is so, there is a conclusion that one must consider: that each one of us is the individual inheritor of seven million years of collective human experience, to the extent that we all now *know*, both literally and metaphorically "in our bones," twined into the DNA itself at this point, that *paying attention to threat is a survival issue.*

This is an important point with regard to using dreams as a support for spiritual development and spiritual guidance - because one of the consequences of this evolutionary experience is that when the deep source within has information of potential use and value to convey to the waking mind, particularly if that information runs counter to some cherished notion or belief, it is very likely to dress that message up in the form of a nightmare, because we are all inherently predisposed to pay more attention to information that comes into our field of awareness in that fashion than we are to pay attention to precisely the same information if it were to come into our field of awareness in some more seemingly benign fashion.

This is why I believe that not only do interesting, "nice," "spiritual" dreams come in the service of health and wholeness and speak a universal language, even the worst, gut-wrenching, sweat-popping nightmares come particularly to serve our health and wholeness. In all the years that I have been working with dreams in America and abroad, with a wide range of folks with different ethnic, religious, and class backgrounds, different gender orientations, in different stages of mental and emotional stability, with different passionately held beliefs, (or none at all), I have never met even a single dream that seemed to me to be saying, "Nyeah, nyeah, nyeah, you've got these problems, and there's nothing you can do about them . . ." This means that *if a dream is remembered at all, it is proof positive that the dreamer is capable of dealing creatively, transformatively, elegantly, effectively, with all the implications the dream raises.*

If the dreamer were not capable of dealing with all of it, the dream simply would not even be remembered. From a spiritual guidance and therapy point of view, this offers a reliable tool for making the difficult judgment call about what the best way to deal with a client at any given moment may be. We are often faced with questions like "Is my responsibility to this person to push him/her forward and urge them onto greater efforts of conscious self-awareness, interior transformation, and change – (Wake up! Smell the coffee! Get on with your life!) – or, is my responsibility more to hold and nurture this person in a nonjudgmental, nondirective, observing, gently supportive presence?" In other words, we are faced regularly with at least these two very different strategies. It is often hard to decide at any given moment which strategy is correct and of most potential use and support to the client.

Over the years, paying close attention to what my clients are dreaming (as well as what I am dreaming myself!), has proved to be an immensely valuable way of evaluating this question. *Is* my client dreaming about the issues that I believe he or she needs to work on? If they are reporting dreams that seem to me, clearly addressing the unresolved psychospiritual issues in their lives, then clearly my responsibility is to urge them forward. If they are *not* remembering dreams around those issues, then it is equally clear that my responsibility is to hold them in a nurturing, non-judgmental, gently observing, embracing presence, without any urging or suggestions about doing anything other than to be who they are and feel what they feel in the moment.

That assessment of any given client may change from one moment to the next, as dreams are shared, and it is the only way I have discovered to make that delicate choice that feels consistently appropriate and professional to me. My colleagues and friends in the various therapy and spiritual guidance fields who have adopted this strategy experimentally, just to see if it works and makes sense for them in their practices, have uniformly reported that this is a very useful principle in making this perennial judgment call — in their own lives, as well as in their work with their clients, patients, and directees. This is one important method for using dreams as a primary source of information and decision making in spiritual guidance with other people.

Not only do all remembered dreams come in the service of health and wholeness, they also all speak a universal language, and that means that, in fact, as a species, we do not lack a single tongue. We do not have to invent Esperanto or Interlingua, or some other type of universal language — we've already got one. The problem with the universal language of the human species is that it is primarily unconscious and primarily symbolic.

Because the language of the dream is universal — because we human beings are inherently predisposed to come up with essentially the same kinds of symbols and metaphors when faced with the same kinds of universal human situations and circumstances, it demonstrates that the health and wholeness that the dreams serve is not limited by the envelope of skin. Yes, every dream does come to serve the health and wholeness of the individual dreamer, but it also comes to serve the health and wholeness of the entire species. Every remembered dream implicates the dreamer as at least a co-participant in, and, I would argue, a co-creator of the larger and larger frameworks of meaning and significance that inhere and are revealed in every dream. By inescapable implication, they come to serve the health and wholeness of the entire ecosystem, because it is ultimately impossible for us to be healthy and whole in an ecosystem that is sick and fragmented. By further implication, they come to serve the health and wholeness of the entire cosmos, which continues to conspire through the functioning of the natural processes of chemistry and physics to preserve the existence of this seemingly unique, little, wet, warm, green place without which we wouldn't even be having this conversation.

Let me stick a quick footnote in here on this word "unconscious." I think, if we were not still groaning under the metaphorical weight of Roman Imperialism, as I believe we still are, we probably would have abandoned the term "unconscious" as our primary technical term a long time ago, because as near as I can make out, the only thing it has to recommend it is that it has been cobbled together from academically fashionable Latin roots. One of the problems of being cobbled together from academically fashionable Latin roots is that people who don't speak Latin, and don't have much respect for academicians believe that anything to do with the "unconscious" is an obscure and obtuse concern, only of interest to people with letters after their names. It has nothing to do with the way ordinary people live their lives. This is a very dangerous misconception.

As a species, we are far more unconscious than we are conscious. The primary determinants of our activities in the world are *unconscious*. But what does that really mean? How can something be "un" and "conscious" all at the same time? There is a phrase out of the Anglo-Saxon word *hoard* that seems to serve our purposes a great deal better. It's the phrase that the Gawain poet and the Pearl poet use to describe both dreaming and the inspired source of poetry. The phrase is "not yet speech-ripe." If, when you hear the word "unconscious" or read the word "unconscious," you try experimentally translating the phrase in your mind as "not yet speech-ripe," I think you will immediately have a much clearer idea about what's going on: there is this stuff inside me and *I have no words for any of it*. Without words, *I can't think about it*. All I know is that it affects my behaviors in ways which moments later I wish it hadn't, but in the immortal words of anyone in this position, "It seemed like a good idea at the time."

What we need with increasing urgency is the ability to put words and images around these unknown parts of our own being that affect the way we think, the way we feel, and most importantly, not just in terms of our individual lives, but also in terms of the planetary community we all share and rely upon, the way we *behave*. Looking at our dreams, particularly with the help of other people, provides a reliable and, in most instances, most enjoyable way of doing this.

My experience as both a dream worker and a community organizer convinces me that Carl Jung was right: we human beings are inherently predisposed to spontaneously represent the most important events of our interior and external lives with essentially the same kinds of symbols, regardless of differences in age, gender, culture, language, passionately held conventions - regardless even of our relative states of emotional and mental stability - and this in turn means that looking at and sharing our dreams with one another is a most reliable and enjoyable technique for promoting the evolution of our conscious self-awareness, particularly in relation to our collective lives, and to the Divine.

This issue of emotional and mental stability also deserves at least a short tangential mention. I am what is known affectionately in the trade as a "red diaper baby." My parents were political radicals. They wrapped me up in the red flag instead of the white diaper, and as a result, I was raised in an atmosphere of absolute conviction that most of the ways that we divide up the human community into the real human beings who are worth trying to get to know and the not-quite-real human beings who are not worth getting to know, are bogus. I was taught that age, race, sex, formal education or the lack of it, and particularly social class were illegitimate ways to divide up the human community, but even I was raised with the idea that there was at least one legitimate way you could divide the community, and that was on the basis of profound mental and emotional disturbance. There were the real human beings who were sane, and the not-quite-real human beings who were crazy, and there was no real point in trying to establish meaningful relationships with crazy people.

Then many years ago I was fortunate enough to be hired as a dream worker in a residential treatment program for psychotic children and young adults in North Berkeley, specifically founded on the clinical insights of Carl Jung, known as St. George Homes, Inc. It was a *great* program. I was there for about twelve years. Although my job description changed wildly the whole time I was there, the thread of continuity through it all was that I did dream work with the kids in the program on a more or less daily basis, and I did dream work with the staff and the volunteers and the visiting firemen and everybody else on a more or less weekly basis. Out of all of those years at St. George, and all of the work I have done prior and subsequently with profoundly disturbed folk, the only real distinction I am able to discover between common garden-variety neurotics, such as ourselves, and those profoundly disturbed psychotics who really should be locked up for their own safety and the safety of the surrounding community, is that we have the luxury of waking up in the morning and asking the universal question "What was that all about?" and they *don't*. It is not the nature of our dreams themselves that separates us; it is our ability to separate ourselves from the reality of our dreams to a certain extent upon waking that makes the key difference.

If you are looking for a functional definition of psychosis, it is (to use currently fashionable Freudian language) when the "object relations" that obtain in the dream world persist without interruption into the waking world — that is to say, when the feelings and ideas that shape the world of the dream world continue to shape the dreamer's waking world unchanged in either emotional intensity or symbolic form. This is the only reliable distinction between neurosis and psychosis that I have been able to discover in all these years of serious work with profoundly disturbed folks.

One thing that follows from this functional definition is that simply sharing dreams with another person can be a profoundly healing experience. Even if you never get to the fascinating question of what all the stuff means, just providing an opportunity for someone to make this distinction between dream experience and the experience of waking life on a regular basis is of immense importance. The goal is to create a space and foster a relationship where the dreamer can say, "This is now, and I'm awake, and one set of reality principles applies. What I'm telling you about was when I was asleep, and another set of reality principles apply . . ." If you can get a profoundly disturbed person to make that distinction on a regular basis, then it is quite likely that any number of other therapeutic interventions will be successful. If you can't get the person to make this distinction on a regular basis, then it is very likely that all the other interventions will fail as well. Simply providing a trustworthy human presence, mirroring and confirming the difference between how I think and feel and behave in the dream world and the potential for how I can think and feel and behave in the waking world is one of the most healing things that we can do for one another.

All dreams are ultimately motivated, in my experience, by an effort to create increasing coherence and wholeness in the dreamer's life harmonizing mind, body, and spirit, unifying soul and psyche. There are many different ways of expressing it, but whatever language structure you use, the dreams are trying to integrate and raise consciousness around the whole system of self and society, so that in addition to the value that comes from the individual parts, a greater value, the value of wholeness itself, generated from its existence as a unified whole. Our lives *are* more than the sum of their parts. The wholeness of our lives creates a different value that is not present when the fragmentation is great, and dreams are always working toward increased integration of the separated and fragmented "parts" and increasing the consciousness of the integration. In this way, all our dreams push us toward an evolving spiritual consciousness, where the parts and the whole truly reflect one another.

By spiritual consciousness I do not mean a restrictive, sectarian religious experience. One of the things that happens in a screenplay I wrote a while back is that at the end, a bunch of characters who have all been evolving more rapidly than the society as a whole are drawn together in a field in Canada, where they all have a shared sense of expectation that some major revelation will happen. One of them turns to one of the others and says, "What do you think is going to happen?" and the person addressed says, "Well, I think the same thing is going to happen that has always happened. Each one of us is going to see what we expect to see, what we have prepared ourselves to see, and then we will be faced with the question: what do we do with the differences in how we perceive this?"

I think that is a high-level archetypal metaphor of the religious and spiritual problem that we face collectively. I come down firmly on the side of breaking down barriers between religious traditions. Regardless of religious difference, a dreamer must recognize that even the nasty, obnoxious dreams are coming in the service of his or her spiritual life, perhaps even more effectively than the beautiful, pastel dreams filled with organ music that everybody automatically thinks is a spiritual dream. To use dreams as a means of guidance to enter the spiritual realms more consciously, one has to be prepared to deal with everything as a symbolic event.

This brings us back to dreams sharing a universal language. One very important example of this is the counter-intuitive archetypal metaphor of "death." Here I am discussing when death appears in the dream world unmasked as "death," not as a symbolic form of a skeleton in a robe with a scythe and an hourglass, but as dead bodies, obituaries in the newspaper, funeral processions, mayhem, or when I flee in the dream because I believe my life is at risk. *Whenever death appears in that literal sense in the dream world, it is the single most frequent and reliable archetypal metaphor of profound psychospiritual growth and change.* I believe the symbol works in this fashion: if I have such a dream it is a very reliable indicator that as the dreamer of this dream, I am engaged in a process of psychospiritual growth and change that is so profound, only the symbolic death of who I used to be, or some aspect of who I used to think I was, is an adequate symbol for the depth of the process that I am engaged in.

But if it is my dream, it is distressing. I don't like it! I wish to wake up from it. And when I wake up from it, I think that was not a nice dream, but in fact, it is one of the highest order dreams celebrating the kind of growth and change that we require and that I am capable of having. Understanding dreams involving death requires us to let go of our white-knuckled grip on our opinions about waking life and receive invaluable information from a less-conscious point of view.

I would like to suggest that the most insidious white-knuckled, fear-driven grip that we all have on our lives is the idea that the real truth about the waking world is that it is a purely material world where rational principles ultimately determine what is going on. We cling to this rationalist, materialist worldview *unconsciously*, even if we are also aware of deep spiritual longings. We live in a world that celebrates the rationalist, materialist world view, and obviously it is effective in producing powerful machines, complicating our lives socially, and eating up all our contemplative time with pressing obligations.

But it is not the whole story. We are forced, when awake, to move around and find our way in a social situation in which operating out of any organizing principle other than rationalist materialism is to risk inviting suspicion, ridicule, and loss of respect. So all of us, no matter how much on our own time we hold onto a larger view, as we run around driving our cars and answering the phone and paying taxes, we operate unconsciously out of that rationalist, materialist worldview. Dreams are constantly asking us to let go of that exclusive view of our lives, and to experience our lives awake in the same multi-leveled, nuanced, symbolic way as we experience and understand our dreams.

I take Carl Jung as my main mentor in this regard, and what I know to be true both as a dream worker and as a community organizer is that the repression and rejection of the archetypal material Jung calls the "shadow "is the primary cause of 99 percent of the misery we visit on one another individually in relationship and collectively in history. The repression and consequent projection of the shadow is a *big* deal. In fact, it is responsible for all the tortures and torments we inflict upon one another, and upon the world as a whole. We reject and deny the dark, problematic aspects of our own being, and then hallucinate that these very factors are the exclusive property of other people. Having denied aspects of our own basic humanity in this process, it is then inevitable and "automatic" — because it is *un*conscious — that we will deny the basic humanity of others, particularly as they have the bad taste to look like the very things we are denying and repressing in ourselves. War, racism, sexism, classism, ageism, pretty-ism, temporarily abledism, even our systematic destruction of the natural environment — all are the direct result of unconscious projection onto others of the archetypal shadow, in whatever particular individual form it takes in each one of us. Repression and projection is, in this very important sense, "the root of all evil."

However, terrible as the consequences are of the repression/projection of the ordinary, "dark" shadow, we are even more diminished by the projection of what is known as "the bright shadow." I know that is saying a mouthful because the projection of the dark shadow is responsible for virtually everything that we can easily and quickly name that is wrong with the world. The failure to own and embrace the bright shadow, and the inevitable unconscious projection of that disowned energy diminishes us in ways that are far less immediately and acutely painful, yet far more profoundly injurious and far more difficult to recognize and overcome.

Let me offer an example, because examples speak a great deal more clearly than theory. Let us suppose for a moment that the great Renaissance artist, Michelangelo, is reincarnated in an upper middle class family in Burlingame, California. His family love him to death, and they put his incredibly talented childhood drawings up on the refrigerator with magnets, and they're community-minded liberals so they send him to public school. But in their secret heart of hearts, they don't think public school is good enough for him, so they send him off to enrichment camp in the summer. He grows up in the lap of love with all of this wealth of support and attention given to him, but unconsciously, and occasionally even consciously, with all the best, good-hearted, loving intentions in the world, he is given the message relentlessly that a career in art is an unacceptable choice for an upper-middle-class male here at the beginning of the twenty-first century. And because the message is delivered to him with love, he *buys it*.

This is a very important point to keep in mind when thinking about dreams and spiritual growth. The oppressions that are delivered with love are much harder to deal with than the oppressions that are delivered with malice. This is because the oppressions that are delivered with malice only require growing up, getting stronger, and acquiring sufficient metaphoric "upper torso strength" to throw them off and overcome them. On the other hand, oppressions that are delivered with love — well, no development of simple emotional upper torso strength is going to be enough to solve that problem. We do not recognize an enemy to fight against. Something else must happen. Now the dreams, bless their hearts, will constantly give us information about what needs to happen, but if it runs counter to our waking ideology, it is a recipe for nightmares.

To get back to the example, let us assume that this is what is happening to our charming young man, and one of the things he has to do as a kid in this situation is to cultivate tremendous self-discipline, because he has to deal constantly with his natural desire to doodle on restaurant napkins and spray paint every blank wall in Burlingame. Because he is so self-disciplined, he does very well in school, but his heart really isn't in any of it. He graduates with straight As, gets a scholarship to Stanford, goes off to university, and does really well there also. He has consistently excellent grades, but has real difficulty picking a major. He picks a liberal arts major because it is the course of least resistance, and he graduates with honors.

Then he decides to go to law school for essentially the same reasons. Because of the diligent work habits he has been cultivating since he was a little boy, he becomes a really good lawyer. He does all kinds of good, pro bono work. He helps build houses for Habitat for Humanity on the weekends. He goes back to Burlingame and marries his high school sweetheart, and they have 1.5 children and a dog. The external view of his life is perfect, and the one thing I can say to you with absolute certainty about this hypothetical character I have created is that his life will be tortured by nightmares — because he is *Michelangelo*, and it just doesn't matter how well he lives somebody else's life. It doesn't even matter how good and public spirited the life is that he's living; it's not the life that his essential being, or, if one chooses to use more traditional language, "God's Will," calls him to do.

Because his repressed passion for art has to go somewhere, he is very likely to become a patron of the arts and to have an extremely good eye picking out young artists before they are famous, buying their art and nurturing them along until they become recognized, and getting even richer in the process. He will be seen by everybody as a pillar of the community and a wonderful guy. When he occasionally secretly goes off to therapy because of his unaccountable struggles with depression and his consistently horrible nightmares, even the therapists will think to themselves, "What the hell is your problem? I would give several fingers off my left hand to have your life. What's the matter with you?!?" Being good Rogerians, one and all, they won't say any of that out loud, but they're thinking it — so, he won't even get genuine sympathy and sensitive help from the very people who are supposedly trained and paid to give it to him. And he will be alone and miserable. But even that sad situation is not the worst thing about this hypothetical situation.

The worst thing about this story, and the real point, is that all of us, the world as a whole, will be deprived of the twenty-first century, even-more-evolved version of the Sistine Chapel. We will be robbed of the twenty-first century version of David, an image that redeems the masculine archetype, which is currently in such desperate need of redemption because the one person in the world who was capable of creating this transformative art didn't do it, *and the rest of us won't even know what we've been robbed of!*

My imaginary reincarnated Michelangelo didn't do what he was deeply called to do for all kinds of "good," socially acceptable reasons, but the result is the same. The world is still bereft of the unique gifts he could have given. In the middle of all of that pain and confusion, the one place that he can turn to, the one part of his complex consciousness he can trust to tell the emotional, psychological, and ultimately spiritual truth about his "exemplary" life, are his dreams.

I believe that Hanna Arandt is right: evil is banal. Even evil geniuses who spend their lives trying to invent new ways of being evil only succeed in creating baroque variations on the ancient, archetypal themes of evil. Anyone who brings his or her own dark shadow into the light of conscious self-awareness and removes the unconscious projections of it from others does a task of world-shaping significance. But there is also always someone else standing right behind that person in line, ready to step forward and project his or her personal and collective shadow, so the world as a whole doesn't appear to change all that much. But the bright shadow is always *unique*. It always offers something that has the potential of changing everything for the better, of raising and evolving the consciousness of the whole species. Once again, the most reliable indications of the state of unconscious denial and projection of both the dark and bright shadow, as well as the potential for more conscious development of these creative energies, can be found in our dreams.

That is why, I believe, dream work and some kind of knowledge of how dreams operate at an archetypal, symbolic level is so important in the practical task of spiritual companioning and building genuine spiritual community. We have to be able to stand naked before one another, and have it all show. We have to be able to accept these increasingly whole, but still incomplete and bloody from metaphorical childbirth, versions of ourselves. We have to be able to accept them from each other and love them in the moment that they are revealed or the community itself will reveal itself to become increasingly false, "fake," and fragile.

Let me use another dream metaphor here: the metaphor of excrement. When excrement appears in folks' dreams there are of course multiple layers of meaning that are likely to inhere in that image at all levels from the uniquely personal to the archetypally collective. At the personal level, the appearance of "shit" is very likely to be a symbolic indication that the dreamer is in the midst of giving up denial. This is because we are all, regardless of gender, culture, language, inherently predisposed to symbolize the worst things about our lives as "shit." The worst things we've ever done, the worst things that other people have ever done to us, the worst things that human beings have ever done at all whether we were there to personally witness it or not, we are inherently predisposed to symbolize all that as excrement. When dung and excrement appear as part of the manifest content of the dream, it is always worth asking: is this dreamer being bludgeoned by circumstances in waking life into giving up some kind of denial about "how bad things actually are"? That is the appropriate question to ask at the immediate personal, relational, psychological level.

At another level, Freud says that shit equals money, and in my experience, he's almost always correct. The argument that he presents to explain symbolic equivalency is that all of us have as our first experience of exerting ourselves physically and producing tangible results the movement of our bowels. That early experience becomes the imprint, the symbolic pattern, for all our efforts in the world to make things happen and produce tangible results and rewards. When excrement appears in a dream, there are almost always levels of symbolic significance having to do with money worries. Freud even suggests that capitalism is, in essence, the inevitable result of premature toilet training. However, my experience is that even though this is very often true, it's also often not that revealing — most of the people who dream about excrement went to bed consciously worried about their finances, and so they don't really need their dreams to tell them that! All dreams have multiple layers of meaning, and this kind of "shit = money" symbol is clearly one of them.

At a larger level, we are all also inherently predisposed to symbolize our spiritual tasks as a kind of "alchemy." We are seeking the transformation of the "base matter" of our lives and experience into the "gold" of reliable spiritual perspective. The basest of base mater is excrement, so the other half of this balanced set of archetypal metaphors is gold. The dream world uses gold very seriously. The archetypal transformation of base matter of our fears and failings into the gold of an adequate spiritual worldview is something all of us must do regardless of our cultural situation. The transformation of shit into gold is an archetypal symbol for spiritual development. Unless we are able to cultivate a spiritual perspective that finds meaning even in the worst things, we will arrive on our deathbeds with the worst things in one hand, because they actually happened, and a spiritual perspective carefully crafted to avoid the worst things in the other. Short of the operations of grace, which simply cannot be predicted, the only possible outcome of that circumstance is hopeless misery and despair.

In order to avoid deathbed misery and despair, while we are alive and energetic enough to do it, we need to give up the denial about the worst things in our lives so they become conscious. Then we are free to think about them, deal with them, and seek the connection to the divine even in the midst of the worst things. The distressing emotional and psychological experience of being forced to give up denial is the necessary first rung of the ladder of authentic spiritual evolution, and when excrement appears in the dream world, it has the quality of a promise that if the dreamer continues to do his or her spiritual work, this excrement will turn into the gold of adequate spiritual perspective and will provide a sense of meaning, even in the midst of authentic suffering.

I think the symbol works like this: all those things that are physically and chemically true about gold in the waking world are symbolically true about adequate spiritual perspective. Its value is intrinsic; it's not relational. A bar of gold lying in the gutter is worth the same amount as a bar of the same weight sitting on the green felt table in the banker's office. The value of gold is inherent. It is immune to rust. It is also immensely malleable. This recalls the difference between spirituality, the gold, and religious tradition, the gold's molded shape. I think all the shapes this gold has been molded into over human history are gorgeous, even the nasty demon shapes.

The last, most difficult piece about understanding dreams and spiritual growth is that we dreamers are uniquely and selectively blind to the deeper meanings of our own dreams, so that in solitude, without the help of others, we are most often unable to see the directions that our dreams are pointing. The problem is that the dreamer is inherently predisposed only to see the levels of dream that reflect things in his or her life of which we are already conscious. It is precisely at the level of innovation and new insight that each dreamer is uniquely and selectively blind. If I can find a community of other dreamers who are willing to listen to my dreams and project on them what they think they could mean, and then have me join the circle to project on their dreams, then we have a way of compensating and overcoming this unique individual, personal blindness that each dreamer is subject to. This is how dream work contributes to spiritual community-building.

I have always believed that anything worthy of the name "salvation," anything that deserves to be called "enlightenment," or "spiritual development," must be a team sport, not an individual championship sport. It is a cooperative, compassionate effort, not a competitive one. Group projective dream work has the potential to be used as way of group spiritual direction and companioning. It allows individuals to overcome our unique and selective psycho-spiritual blindness and to cultivate intimate connections with one another that nurture and support deep evolving, vital, and alive spiritual community.

This collective energizing of spiritual awareness and cultivation of emotional and psychological maturity that regularly manifests when people share dreams together, one-to-one, and in groups, is one of the primary reasons I have devoted the last forty years of my personal and professional life to promoting group projective dream work. It is a way of building and strengthening community and individual relationships. It is an authentic spiritual discipline, as well as a dynamic technique for promoting therapy and healing. It can be practiced as an entertainment activity for consenting adults, as a way of companioning the dying, on their final journey, as well as companioning the living in their grief and suffering. It is an immensely successful way of inspiring the young, and a way of awakening and releasing the archetypal creative impulse that is our most important heritage as human beings. As the sign on the carnival merry-go-round at the end of Orson Wells's wonderful, allegorical film, *Lady from Shanghai*, says: "There is no limit to the speed of this machine."

Spiritual Intimacy

Recently I had the opportunity to dialog with his Holiness the Dalai Lama, Bishop Tutu, Judge Shirin Ebadi (the Nobel Prize winner from Iran), and Professor Joan Archibald, who spoke as the representative of indigenous Canadian people. I asked four important questions of this group.

First: What ideas of cosmology do we need in order to approach the healing of the planet? Clearly, the reality map we have at this time is not productive for life and health. Creativity does not reside in the way we are imprisoned to repeat precedent. It is in daring — to be outrageous, to play with the least probable possibilities, the ones more weird and spiritual, where we may find answers. These possibility forms dance before the mind's eye and from that vision there emerges an unexpected form with its creative proposal for a new way to understand and map reality. We need to learn this process of creative questing in order to discover the cosmology that will help us approach the healing of the planet.

Second: What is the basic health ethos arising from that new cosmology? The cosmology of the industrial revolution gave us an ethos to productivity at any cost. The cosmology of corporate capitalism pushes an ethos to consumption at any cost. The cosmology we seek to find should produce first and foremost an ethos that honors harmonious biological health in the individual and in the environment. In order to co-create this cosmology we can no longer rely on the insights of a single mind. The complexity, and with it the responsibility, of what we have to achieve in the world is too great to bear for only one person. The only way to get it together is to do it together.

I plead for research that would discover what it takes to enable us to operate in webs of consciousness, in networks of shared minding. I desire at least for a small group of prepared minds to seek to merge dreams and behold visions. These people would serve as our psycho-nauts and contact minds on other regions. We are quite underdeveloped in this area. We have very basic ideas of how groups really work. While there is immense sophistication in the technological area of military systems and lethal weapons of mass destruction, we lack understanding of how to handle conflict resolution. Much research needs to be done to help us move toward optimal social and political harmony, and this cannot wait.

I have often challenged educators to plan their curricula for handling information with ecological wisdom, for the formation of character, for education of the heart, for raising the emotional IQ, for teaching skills of cooperation that would produce the adepts, saints, zaddikim, rishis, bodhisattvas and shamans that we need at this time.

Third: What are the *upaya*, the skillful means, needed to lift cultural trance and launch the awareness of the emerging cosmology? The mind of the current consensus leads us to ever greater crises. We must do the miraculous work of transforming the awareness of millions of people. We must go deeper and deeper into regions where we cannot use muscle effort, where only awareness can shift awareness. One of my friends calls this changing the tires while the car is moving, and our planet's car is moving fast. We need to update the inner resources of our spiritual traditions that once worked well, but are associated with a flesh-rejecting monastic asceticism. If a teacher's suggestions for my spiritual practice exceed twenty minutes in the morning and twenty minutes in the evening, I will not do them. The old traditions demand more time than I can afford. We need to look at what works of the old techniques and enhance their yield by learning to attune our consciousness to optimal transformational power. These actions take place in other regions than the mind of the shopping mall. When I think of the turbulent mind space we inhabit at this time, I get close to experiencing schizophrenia. I can't hear the choral — symphonic music of a sacred common dream. Just as some people once lamented the twilight of the gods, so it seems that we now experience the twilight of the life-affirming archetypes. How can we access them? How can we empower them? How can they empower us? We have come to realize that we are not on the top of the chain of being. What do we, as spiritual people, have as means to access the waiting helpers from higher planes? When I was at Dharamsala, the Dalai Lama and I started to talk about angels. They were a reality for him as they are for us, but most people have no sense of beings near the top of the scale of the conscious evolution. Only when we gain understanding of the deep life process can we embark on designing the needed education of heart and spirit.

Last: What adjustments in psychology, anthropology, biology, physics, medicine, philosophy, political science, theology, spiritual technologies, economics, the arts, communications, and most of all, ethics do we need in order to heal the planet? The big questions remain. The current state of the disciplines of transpersonal psychology and Transpersonal Sociology are too primitive to handle our crisis. I asked these questions of my colleagues, and now I invite you to help find the answers with us.

When I was asking these questions, as a real subtext I was actually asking: is there a curriculum for bodhisattvas? Our educational system is not trying to help them out. The "indigo" children who are now being born and other amazing healer souls are not offered ways to be educated and raised in a system where they would be developed spiritually.

What is it that we have to do to bring transpersonal psychology up to date? Jorge Ferrer has done wonderful work on revisioning the theory of transpersonal psychology. He makes a very important point, which is that any epistemology with which we are operating today has to be a *participatory epistemology*. This means it is not that we know something that is outside of us, but rather, we are part of the knowledge system. We have to bring this into transpersonal psychology, that we ourselves are part of the picture, part of the system of knowledge.

I would like to see some research with shamans, who exemplify this participatory epistemology; alas they do not articulate it well as such.

Many of them are very good, great spiritual geniuses, but they may not have the language to teach what they know. I have met some beautiful holy ones who have come from South America, who do great rituals and are able to have great power, who operate from deeply spiritual regions. But the question for us will remain: what are those spiritual regions? How do you get into them? Is there a way to open up channels so that we do them with the *upaya*, the skillful means? Transpersonal psychology can upon intensive effort and research make that discipline, that knowledge, available to us.

In the more subtle regions it is important to work as an ensemble. That is to say, to go into those regions without going crazy, you must have friends who are going to be with you, who will support the work, and who will be able to monitor you. One of our Hassidic masters wrote a letter to a friend of his. He said, "I watched on the way up, and you did very well. On the way down, you made a couple of mistakes. Let me tell you what they were." The master guided his friend, so that the friend would be able to do better the next time. In a shamanic journey, it is important to have more than one person go there. Alone, there is not the consensual revelation that is necessary to give us a sense of deeper reality that comes when a group works together.

There is something that happens in the dialog between the master and the disciple. It is called *yehidut* in Hassidism. It has its counterpart in spiritual direction in Christianity, *mondo* in Zen, *darshan* in Hinduism, *sohbet* in Sufism.

When I look at spiritual direction in history, I recognize that it took people a lot of time and motivation to go deeply into transformation. Very often, the people who come to transpersonal psychologists at this point are looking for crisis intervention and for ways in which they can use and access their spirituality to help them through the crisis. In other words, they are looking for invisible means of support in order to be able to do the holy work that they have to do.

Historically, we had a shared understanding: it was taken for granted that the priest, minister, guru, or sheikh was on a much, much higher level than the student. This hierarchical stance is still true in some practices. When I see some of the gurus who come from India with their retinue, there is a strong hierarchical order by which they are perceived. But even that arrangement does not capture the deep sense of deference a student would feel in many ancient systems of spiritual guidance. There was an understanding that the teacher had the answers and the disciples, the supplicants, were the ones who came with the questions.

In our day, we cannot prescribe for people in such a way. We cannot be the guru, the rabbi, or the sheikh in the paradigm in which there was that hierarchical deference. As Alan Watts used to say, there are two types of gurus. There is a *sat guru*. He knows where it's at. There is an *upa guru* who just says, "I know the tools that you need to use." We are in the situation of the *upa guru*. That is to say, people nowadays don't come to us to tell them where it's at because we all believe they have to find it out for themselves. What they come to us for is method. They are asking us: how do I go about doing that which I need to do in order to overcome the difficulties in my life and in order to reach higher?

A nun once told me so beautifully: "Spiritual direction deals with only one thing: how to reduce our resistance to God." Once we manage to reduce our resistance, we are in a much better place because we are connected, and that connection inspires us and guides us. To live under guidance is to live in a situation where the universe responds to us and informs whether we are on the right track or not. For that, we have to reduce our resistance to God.

Many of us get to be so busy in helping people that sometimes we are not doing enough soul maintenance for ourselves. Many times when we give people directions on how to meditate, we give them directions that look like swimming a racing stroke. All of that is very strongly ego driven. I suggest we give them backstroke meditation. The difference between them is that in the backstroke meditation, you have to relax. You have to allow the water to hold you. At the same time you can move, but your movement is a lot more into, if you will, the *Cloud of Unknowing*, into the not-knowing space. Everything we know, we know from the past. What we need to know is not in the past, it is in the future. Backstroke swimming is helpful if you can translate it to your meditation. I quote a sentence from the Song of Songs, "Draw me after you, let us make haste. The King has brought me into his chambers."[5] In other words, it is not likely that we can go into the deeper and higher places if we do the steering that comes from ego direction.

We therefore need, for our own maintenance, to be able to do that kind of meditation and to reduce our own resistance to God. Very often it happens that in a session of spiritual direction, in that spiritual intimacy, if we are not vulnerable and open, the other one is going to feel it. It feels immediately to them that you are trying to take the higher moral and knowledge ground, and you are talking down to the person you are with. When you are doing your own backstroke meditation, and are letting go of your own ego direction, you are more available for spiritual intimacy with others.

At the same time that we are doing our practice alone, we must also practice with friends. Before every Rosh Hashana High Holy Day, I sit with three of my friends and ask them, "What have you seen this year in me that I really need to know? I'm so busy with the presentation of myself I can't see clearly. You see me better. Tell me what you see." When friends answer you, and you are open to it, it helps your own spiritual maintenance. Sometimes friends have to say something that is a bit harsh. Yet at the same time, there is a deep truth in it, because it comes from intimacy. I think it is not enough to have people meet with you in the consultation room. You need to have groups with whom you do some rituals and celebrations, and so do your clients. It is necessary that you prepare yourself spiritually for counseling, and asking your friends to talk with you in this way can be very helpful. Of course, there are other ways of preparing yourself for the task of guiding others, and we are all familiar with being students and using our course of study as preparation. One of my great mentors was Howard Thurman who was the dean of the chapel at Boston University, a very great and holy soul. He gave a course in spiritual discipline and resources, and

I was eager to take the course. The class was important for me because we participated in labs, not just lectures. In other words, the class wasn't just talking; it was trying meditation out so that we could replicate it on our own. We were trying to do the inner work at the same time as learning the techniques. We asked, "Who am I at the end of the day, and what have I done in my examination of consciousness?" Howard Thurman didn't want to come into a lab without having a couple of hours of preparation for himself, so he could be in the vibration he needed to be able to transfer to us. He needed that preparation because it is so difficult to teach students anything about doing inner work.

It turns out that we have good language for reason and sensation, but we have a very poor vocabulary for intuition and feeling. For example, these are common phrases: I'm feeling low; I'm feeling high; I'm feeling bitter; I'm feeling sweet. We say things like: I have a dark feeling; I have a light feeling. We borrow words from sensations to talk about feelings.

Because we don't have a good vocabulary for what happens in intuition, there are many times when you sit down with somebody in counseling and something uncomfortable comes up in you, and you don't know where it came from. It doesn't fit anything you have dealt with in the past so you begin to doubt yourself. Can you trust your intuition in that moment? Intuition needs to be developed. It needs to be reinforced.

This is where the teachings of Vedanta, Hassidism, Kabbalah, Buddhism, and Sufism are so important because they give the mind the wherewithal to wrap itself around what the soul knows. The soul knows what your intuition tells you, but your mind often can't grasp anything paradoxical, or oxymoronic. The more you read spiritual direction literature, the more you can learn ways to help the mind grasp what the soul knows. Once that has happened, you can communicate your intuition to people.

As you practice this awareness, you also are asking your clients to practice it. Practically, this can mean asking some questions in an early counseling session. You can ask a person with whom you are working,

"What is your religious background? What is your religious preference? How do you pray?" One of the things that Howard Thurman
asked me was to show him what my prayer life was all about.

I think spirituality is one of the issues most important to intake
sessions. Most people report some kind of practices. They say, "I do
a little tai chi and a little aikido, and I do some Vipassana, and I do a
little of this and a little of that." Then you say, "How often do you do
it?" They say, "Well, you see, I have to spend some quality time with
my family. I'm not . . . you know . . ." Then you say, "How much quality time do you spend with the family?" Then they reply, "I'm not
together enough . . . I'm not together enough . . ."

At that point I suggest to people that they should begin to socialize
their meditation. It is a very important thing to find a friend for the
person whom you counsel. There are some times when you get into
that place where you come as a spiritual friend to your session. That
is one way to offer spiritual direction. The risk of it is that certain
demands can end up being made on you that would normally be made
on friends, and your time is no longer your own. People will take it for
granted that you are friends, and then get disappointed that you are
still a professional and a person who is doing this as a vocation.

So it is important that you ask people to have a friend with whom
they can discuss their sessions. It can be wonderful if the friend also
comes sometimes into the spiritual direction with a fresh perspective.
Then your client and their friend can help each other. Spiritual intimacy comes from harnessing soul knowledge and being able to
express it to another person. You can help make sure your clients are
practicing this outside of their sessions with you by suggesting they
cultivate spiritual intimacy with their friends.

Another very important skill to practice and teach is awareness of
how you can use your body to reinforce your spiritual lessons. This is
necessary both for someone offering spiritual guidance and for the
person receiving it. When I went to my master, I would enter the consultation room with a great deal of humility. I would kiss the mezuz-
zah at the door, walk in to see him, and by the time I stood in front of

him, I was concave, hollow, actively receptive. He was convex. I wanted to get to that place inside of me where I would get the maximum signal from him. The maximum signal didn't only come with words. It came with his vibrational atmosphere. Later on when I tried to enter into prayer and meditation, that vibratory place that I could recall from my body, which I learned from my master intuitively, was very helpful. Rabbi Nahman of Bratzlav said it very beautifully. Teach your body every spiritual lesson. The mind and the soul, they will change. If you learn in your body, then when you need to recall the lesson, it will be sitting there in the body, and you can bring it up from there.

I will end with a little story about spiritual intimacy. The incarnation of the Ba'al Shem Tov, before he came to be a Ba'al Shem Tov, was a very simple shoe patcher. One day Elisha the prophet came to him in the middle of the night and said, "I have been sent from heaven to find out what it is that you did on the day of your bar mitzvah that gave God such pleasure that God didn't hasten the destruction of the temple."

The shoe patcher heard this question, and he said, "If God didn't tell you, I won't tell you either." Prophet Elijah said, "If you tell me, I will teach you the secrets of the Torah." The shoe patcher replied, "I'm not interested in that. What I did was for God alone."

Elijah left, and all the saints in heaven asked, "What did he say? What did he say?" Elijah explained that the shoe patcher didn't want to tell what he had done. Angered, the saints wanted to send thunderbolts down on him, but Prophet Elijah said, "You don't understand. He gave you something much deeper than if he had told you what he did. He has taught you that what you do, you do for God alone."

All of our work toward spiritual intimacy with each other is ultimately work toward intimacy with God. What you do, you do in the presence not just of each other, but in the presence of God.

Spiritual Guidance in the Sufi Tradition

The great Sufi saint Abdul Qadir al-Jilani wrote, "Your heart is a polished mirror. You must wipe it clean of the veil of dust which has gathered upon it, because it is destined to reveal divine truths."[6] We cannot dust anyone else's mirror for them. As spiritual guides, we can encourage others to do the cleaning for themselves. And, according to the Sufi tradition, when we begin to wipe off a few grains of dust, God cleans the rest.

The term "Sufi" has several root meanings in Arabic, including "purity" and "wool." Sufis seek outer and inner purity, and the early Sufis wore simple, patched woolen cloaks. Another root meaning is "line" or "row." At the time of the Prophet, there were a group of devoted Muslims who sat in a row in front of his house in Medina. They accompanied him whenever they could, and it is said that this group received spiritual instruction from the Prophet and were the first Sufis.

Those who practice Sufism are known as "Sufis," or "dervishes," a Persian word related to "door" or "doorway." Many early Sufis were wandering mendicants who came to the doors of householders to receive food and shelter. Also, a dervish stands at the threshold between the material and spiritual worlds, constantly seeking to enter more fully the spiritual realm. Another associated term is "fakir," from the Arabic word "poverty." This refers to spiritual poverty, including a simple lifestyle and lack of attachment to the things of this world.

I met my Sufi master in 1980. At that time, I was the president of the Institute of Transpersonal Psychology, a psychology graduate school I founded in 1975. Sheikh Muzaffer Ozak came to my school as a guest teacher.

The day he arrived I was sitting in my office talking on the telephone. Someone walked past my office; I had no idea who he was. The man looked at me as he walked by. He simply glanced at me and kept walking, but when he looked at me, time stood still. In that timeless moment, I felt as if all the data of my life was sent instantly into an enormous computer, and that the computer effortlessly integrated everything and understood how my life had been and how it was going to turn out. Then the thought came to my mind, "Who was that man? I hope that was the Sufi master we invited, because if that was just one of the dervishes, I don't think I'm ready to meet the sheikh."

That was how I met my spiritual teacher. Sheikh Muzaffer was the head of the Halveti-Jerrahi Order, a three hundred-year-old branch of an eight hundred-year-old Order. Our mother center is in Istanbul, which has one foot in Asia and one foot in Europe, a city that joins together East and West. This ancient mystical tradition has been the core of my spiritual life for more than twenty five years.

I have been a teacher in this tradition for more than twenty years. Spiritual guidance in our tradition is somewhat different from most other forms of spiritual guidance. I work with a small Sufi community of about thirty-five dervishes. We meet together three times a week, and over the past twenty-five years we have gotten to know each other very well.

Our order often works with dream analysis, and I spend a good deal of time listening to and interpreting the dervishes' dreams and discussing the interpretations with them. I also practice what I call "one-minute spiritual guidance," which consists of short, informal check-in conversations with members of my community during dinner, over tea, on the telephone, or through e-mail. For guidance in greater depth, I generally meet with dervishes individually for up to an hour or more.

Spiritual guidance in our tradition has two major elements I will discuss here. One is work in cleansing and transforming the personality, and the other is opening the heart.

Transforming the Personality

Working to transform oneself is known as the inner *jihad*, or inner struggle. The Qur'an often uses the term jihad in the context of "struggle in the way of God." Once, the Prophet was riding back to Medina after the battle of Badr. The Muslim warriors were overjoyed that they had managed to defeat their attackers against great odds. Then the Prophet commented, "Now we are going to the greater jihad!" The warriors were exhausted and many were wounded. They could not imagine fighting another battle. The Prophet told them, "The greater jihad is the struggle with what is in your breast."

The inner jihad is often described as the struggle against our *nafs*, or our egos. The Arabic word *nafs* has various meanings, including "essence" and "breath." The most common meaning for *nafs* in Arabic is "self," although it can also be translated as "ego" or "soul." The *nafs* is essentially our sense of separate individuality, which keeps us separate from God. The self can be thought of as having more than one level, and as one moves through these levels one comes closer and closer to union with God.

The Tyrannical Self

The lowest level is the *nafs ammaara*, or the tyrannical self. It is referred to in the Qur'an as the self that continually commands or incites us to do evil. The root verb is *amara*, to command. It is often used in the Qur'an, for example, "God commands us to pray and do good works." The variant *ammaara* is a more intense verb form. God has given us free will, and we can choose to follow or to reject God's commands. On the other hand, the tyrannical self seeks to take away our free will, to dominate us and blind our eyes to truth.

The tyrannical self is a collection of all those inner forces that lead us away from doing God's will. The core of the tyrannical self is our sense of separateness plus narcissism or excessive self-love. The tyrannical self tries to convince us we are better and more important

than everyone else, and that we do not need to follow anyone or anything, not even God.

In the Sufi tradition, this narcissistic, self-centered, egocentric level
of the self is our great enemy on the spiritual path. Yet the ego can also
be an invaluable instrument for our work in the world. Part of our job
is to transform the ego, not to kill it. Without the ego, we cannot do
very much.

Freud pointed out that the ego is a valuable tool to help us cope with
the world. According to Freud, the ego develops as our perceptual
capacities develop. One of the main jobs of the ego is to mediate between
the blind cravings of the id and the realities of the world around us.

However, in his writings, Freud may have focused on the wrong
Greek myth. Instead of the myth of Oedipus, we should reflect more
deeply on the legend of Narcissus. Sufi psychology points to narcissism as the greatest core problem we face, both spiritually and psy-
chologically. It is the narcissistic ego that we are trying to transform.

The story goes as follows: Narcissus was an extraordinarily hand-
some young man. Many young men and women fell in love with him,
but he rejected them all. The nymph Echo also fell in love with
Narcissus. She had been cursed by Hera because she distracted Hera
with her chatter while Hera was trying to discover which of the
nymphs was having an affair with Hera's father, Saturn. Hera cursed
Echo, saying, "You will always have the last word, but no power to
speak first." As a result, Echo could only repeat what others said and
never speak for herself.

Echo followed Narcissus into the hills. He heard her in the trees and
asked, "Is anyone here?" Echo responded, "Here." Narcissus said,
"Come," and Echo replied, "Come." Narcissus said, "Be with me." Echo
ran out and embraced him, saying, "Be with me." Then Narcissus
pushed her away, exclaiming, "I will die before I give you power over
me." Echo answered, "I give you power over me." But Narcissus
refused even her love.

Eventually, one rejected young woman prayed to the Goddess
Nemesis that Narcissus would experience the pain of unrequited love,

which he had caused to so many others, and Nemesis cursed him with overwhelming self-love. Narcissus became so fascinated by his own reflection that he could not stop gazing at his image, and he starved to death. We might ask ourselves and those we guide why we are so fascinated by our false, inflated self-images, to the extent we are in danger of starving to death, emotionally and spiritually.

The tyrannical self is often symbolized by the Pharaoh, who refused to free the children of Israel. The Pharaoh was not only the ruler of Egypt; he was also worshipped as a god. Our narcissistic ego wants to be revered as well, and this worship of another "god" in place of God is considered the greatest sin in Islam.

At the level of the tyrannical self, we are like addicts in denial, dominated by self-love and narcissism and unable to recognize that we have a serious problem. Our addiction to praise and fame is, in many ways, a more difficult addiction than drugs and alcohol. We want everyone to notice us and think well of us. We always want more, and nothing is good enough for us.

We all have to struggle with the impulses of our tyrannical self. Those who believe they need not be concerned with these powerful forces run the risk of becoming dominated by the tyrannical self. Many harmful, evil acts are committed by those who rationalize their behavior as righteous, or even religious. Although the tyrannical self is described as the first stage of the self, it can also be considered as a set of egotistical, arrogant tendencies in us, tendencies that continue to affect us throughout our lives, even as we progress along the spiritual path.

The Regretful Self

The second level is the regretful self. At this stage, we begin to see more clearly the power of our egos; we are no longer in denial and we know we have to fight the inner jihad. However, old habits die hard, and we often continue to behave selfishly or hurtfully in spite of our new found awareness. We are motivated to keep trying to change by our regret over our past harmful actions. This stage requires patience and perseverance. The inner jihad really begins at this stage. At the first stage, the tyrannical self, there is very little struggle because our unconsciousness and rationalization are so strong.

The narcissistic ego is like a thief who sneaks into your house at night, seeking to steal whatever is valuable in your life. You wake up (a sign of the stage of the regretful self) and hear the thief enter, but you know the thief has the capacity to mirror your actions. If you pick up a gun, the thief will have a gun also. If you take a knife, the thief will have a knife. You are likely to kill each other if you try to fight the thief. So what do you do?

The answer is: turn on the lights. If the house is suddenly filled with light, the thief will flee, because the thief is a coward who relies on working in the dark. In the inner jihad of the regretful self, we focus the light of self-awareness on the tendencies of the tyrannical self. The more we are aware of our negative tendencies, the weaker they become. Also, as we develop spiritually, the soul's light increases and the power of the tyrannical self weakens.

The Inspired Self

Initial success at the inner jihad brings us more in touch with our souls, with our own inner light and wisdom. We reach a new level of understanding based on the spiritual inspiration and discernment that come from within.

Sufi masters warn that the inspired self is actually one of the most dangerous spiritual stages. The ego is still very much intact, and it will try and claim our inner insight and wisdom as its own. There is serious danger of ego inflation and spiritual narcissism. The great Sufi master Bayazid Bistami commented, "The thickest veils between man and God are the wise man's wisdom, the worshiper's worship, and the devotion of the devout." This is one of the reasons the Sufis insist on the importance of a sheikh or spiritual guide who can help us recognize our tendency toward spiritual inflation.

Although the individual is not free of the ego, its power is significantly reduced. The struggle at this stage is to *practice* our highest values, to live by what we believe in.

The Serene Self

At this stage the individual has overcome the ego's unending need for recognition and gratification and has become content with whatever he or she has in this world. The seeker is no longer driven by the need for more possessions and greater recognition. This newfound serenity is our foundation for a real spiritual life.

Most of us are rarely content with our lives. Even on vacation, we are often dissatisfied with the food in the restaurants or with the service in the hotel. We miss the comforts of home when we are on vacation, and we long for a vacation when we are at home. We are almost always unhappy with the present, hoping something special will happen in the future.

Our constant desire for more is illustrated in one of my favorite Sufi stories, the merchant and the Sufi. A wealthy merchant saw a Sufi praying in the mosque. The merchant was inspired by the devotion of the Sufi, and when the Sufi finished his prayers, the merchant went over and gave him a bag of gold coins saying, "Please take this money and use it to help others. I am sure that you will do more good with it than I would."

The Sufi replied, "I am not sure I can take your money. It would not be right to deprive you or your family. Do you have more money at home?"

The merchant proudly claimed, "I have over a thousand gold pieces at home!"

"Do you pray to God for even more gold?" the Sufi asked.

"Yes, of course. Every day I pray that God might increase my wealth."

The Sufi handed the bag of gold back to the merchant. "I cannot take your money. A wealthy man cannot take money from a beggar."

The merchant was shocked. After all, he was the wealthy one and the Sufi was the beggar. Then the Sufi explained, "I am wealthy because I am content with whatever God sends me, and you are the beggar because, in spite of all you have, you are constantly begging God for more."

Those who attain the level of serenity live in the present moment. The Prophet said, "There is no prayer without the presence of the heart." For real prayer we have to be both present and openhearted. Real dervishes are not lost in fantasies of a better future or unending desire for more possessions or greater fame.

The Pleased Self

At this stage the individual welcomes even the trials and difficulties of life, knowing that all things come from God. According to psychology, most people spend their lives seeking pleasure and avoiding pain. This makes them puppets of the ever-changing world around them. The Sufis who have reached the stage of the pleased self look only to God and are beyond the influence of their material surroundings.

This stage is well illustrated in the Sufi story of Ayaz and the cucumber. Ayaz was a deeply devoted follower of Sultan Mahmud of Ghazna, and the sultan loved him as a son. One day the two were sitting together eating lunch. The sultan cut a slice of cucumber and gave it to Ayaz, who ate it with relish. A little later he gave another slice of cucumber to Ayaz and took one for himself. When Mahmud bit into the cucumber, he immediately spit it out as it tasted terrible— chalky and bitter. He looked angrily at Ayaz and exclaimed that Ayaz had tricked him into eating that bitter cucumber by pretending it was delicious.

Ayaz answered, "No, my sultan. It was delicious to me. I have received so many wonderful things from your hand, that whatever comes from you is sweet to me."

When we feel the same love and gratitude to God that Ayaz felt toward his sultan, whatever comes to us will seem sweet, and we will have attained the stage of the pleased self.

The Self Pleasing to God

At this stage the Sufis have achieved inner unity and wholeness. This is the stage of the inner marriage of the soul and the self. The self is now in the service of God, no longer a hindrance on the spiritual path. Those who have attained this stage have become single-hearted and single-minded. They have become real Muslims as they have now completely submitted themselves to God's will.

The great Sufi poet Jelaluddin Rumi writes that most people cannot experience God all around them because they experience the world as multiplicity instead of unity. A broken mirror creates a thousand reflections of a single image. At this stage, our inner nature is made whole and we can experience God's unity all around us.

The Pure Self

Few attain this final level, perhaps only the greatest prophets and saints. They have transcended the self entirely. There is no ego, no sense of separateness left, only union with God. They have fully realized the truth of "There is no god but God." Only God exists for them. There is nothing other than God, and any sense of individuality or separation is an illusion.

Rumi beautifully describes this state:

> If you could get rid
> of yourself just once,
> the secret of secrets
> would open to you.
> The face of the unknown,
> hidden beyond the universe,
> would appear on the mirror of your perception.[7]

Opening the Heart

In the Sufi tradition, the heart is alive. The spiritual heart is in reality an active, vibrant process; it is not a thing. One of our most important jobs in spiritual guidance is to pay attention to the spiritual heart. Our heads are generally over-educated and over-developed, and we all need to begin to think more with our hearts, feel with our hearts, and know with our hearts.

The word "courage" comes from the French word for heart, *coeur*. Courage is the power of the heart, the power of will and commitment. It is the power of inner strength, not merely muscular strength. An athlete with "heart" has this kind of strength. The heart is the place of passion and intensity.

In the Sufi tradition, the heart is the place of imagination and creativity. One of my Sufi teachers once said, "The head is like a computer. It remembers things. It can generate thoughts but it is not really creative, any more than a computer is creative. Creativity comes from the heart." Understanding comes from the heart. Poetry, art, and music come from the heart.

Many years ago a Sufi teacher was recuperating from an illness. His devoted follower would get up before dawn and heat water for the teacher's morning ablutions. One winter morning the student got up and found his teacher was already awake. He grabbed a pitcher of ice-cold water and held it tight against his breast. When he began to pour the water over his teacher's hands, it was scalding hot. Amazed, the teacher asked his beloved follower, "Where did you boil this?" The follower replied, "On the fire of my heart, my master."

The physical heart is a fascinating analog to the spiritual heart. According to Aristotle and many early Sufi masters who were also accomplished physicians, the heart is the central organ in the body. According to Ibn Sina (Avicenna), the heart is the organ that actually represents the entire body because it is the center of the circulatory system. The heart sends blood to every organ and every cell of the body. It is, in a sense, the integrative organ of the body. The physical heart and the circulatory system nourish every cell, and also carry away waste products from the cells and purify them. Similarly, the spiritual heart nourishes every aspect of our psyche and also purifies our psyche. The heart is our inner spiritual guide.

A detailed Sufi model of the heart was written by Al-Tirmidhi, an eighth century mystic, scholar, and physician. He was born in Khorasan, in what is now Northeastern Iran, on the Silk Road. Khorasan was a great center of civilization and culture for many centuries. Al-Tirmidhi described four levels of the heart. His model provides one compelling way of describing the process of spiritual guidance as the work of heart opening.

The Breast

The first level is the breast, or the outermost heart. The breast is called *sadr* in Arabic, and it means heart and mind combined. In many languages, the heart and mind are thought of as a single entity. The word *sadr* also means to go out, to lead, and to resist or oppose. The breast lies between the heart proper and the ego, which is our instrument of action in the world. The breast is the place of the purification and transformation of the tyrannical self, or narcissistic ego.

The breast is the place in which we work on the transformation of the self, seeking to convert the ego from narcissistic starvation to aliveness, prayer, and service. My master, Sheikh Muzaffer, said, "Understand that every action affects your outermost heart. Every kind word, every kind glance, and every kind act softens the heart and opens the heart. And every mean word, every harmful act closes the heart." He added, "Your actions affect not only your own heart. Every kind word, every kind glance causes a rose or a flower to bloom somewhere. Every unkind act causes a thorn to grow."

If we understand this, the world offers abundant opportunities for spiritual practice. Every interaction is a spiritual encounter. If I behave kindly, my heart opens, and if I can help open another's heart, we both gain a rich spiritual reward. One basic Sufi practice is to remember that the heart of everyone we meet is a temple that houses the divine spark within each of us. This means to behave with remembrance that God is located within the heart of hearts in each individual.

Then, each encounter is a prayer. Each encounter is worship. In Arabic, the words worship and service have the same roots. *'Ibadet* is Arabic for worship, and *'abd* is servant. When we truly serve each other, we are worshipping God. The great psychologist Alfred Adler said, many years ago, "I can cure any neurosis. It's very simple—just get people to help other people. If you get people to behave unselfishly, their neurotic problems will go away."

The Heart Proper

The second level of the heart is the *qalb,* or the heart proper. In Arabic, *qalb* is related to the notion of a banner blowing in the breeze. It is constantly moving; like radar constantly scanning the environment, the spiritual heart is constantly looking for God.

The heart is the source of our inner knowledge, as opposed to acquired knowledge. Acquired knowledge includes whatever we learn from anything outside ourselves—from books, teachers, friends. But there is another kind of knowledge, the knowledge of the heart. The head holds acquired knowledge, but the heart holds inner knowledge. We need to develop this inner wisdom, which is the core of our ability of discernment. We need to nourish the inner wisdom in those we work with.

The spiritual heart is also the place of intention. According to a famous saying of the Prophet, "Actions are according to intentions." The intention of the heart gives meaning to all our actions. The intention of the heart shapes the meaning and the results of all we do. If we reflect deeply we may find our intensions are mixed or unclear. Part of the Sufi tradition of spiritual guidance is to help others clarify their intentions. I often ask those I guide, "What do you want to happen? What is the deepest desire of your heart? What do you want in your life? What do you think God wants you to do?" I have found that clarifying our intentions will often lead us toward what we want.

The Inner Heart

The third level of the heart is called *fuad* in Arabic. It is the place of vision in us. In one sense, the heart knows and this inner heart sees. Seeing is deeper than knowing. For example, if I tell you about a foreign city and you have never been there, I can describe it in great detail, but that is not at all like going there and seeing it for yourself.

There is an immediacy about seeing something instead of merely hearing about it. Seeing means to experience something firsthand. Most of our spiritual experiences occur at the level of the inner heart.

We serve as guides for people who are seeking deeper spiritual experience. How do we discuss these experiences with those we are guiding? How can we help them honor and also articulate their spiritual experience? The inner heart is a place where we can be aware of God's presence. It is the place of remembrance, the place of knowledge of God's presence. It is a sacred place within us.

The Innermost Heart

The fourth level is the innermost heart, or the heart of hearts. It is the place of our most profound spiritual experience, the experience of unity.

When Tirmidhi describes this level, his writing style changes radically. He switches from prose to poetry, from logical and linear discussion to metaphor and parable. This seriously disturbed me when I was trying to develop his model in a book on Sufi psychology. I said to myself, "Wait a minute, Tirmidhi, you were really clear and logical in describing the first three levels, why are you becoming unclear and allegorical now?" I now realize he would probably answer, "How else can I describe what is beyond logic and beyond our limited rationality?" Tirmidhi describes the innermost heart in terms such as "The innermost layer of the heart is God's garden. It is irrigated with the water of God's mercy and compassion." I eventually gave up my attempts to write about the innermost heart in a logical and rational matter, and I ended up quoting Tirmidhi's wonderful poetry and metaphors.

The heart of hearts is that within us which is infinite in scope and which is infinite in radiance. My Sufi master said, "That divine spark which is located in our heart of hearts could set fire to the entire known universe, because it is greater than the universe that surrounds us."

Sufi practice is meant to lead us toward the experience of unity, and also to teach us to live with the awareness that God is always present in our heart of hearts. My Sufi master once commented that the highest calling in the world is to heal the human heart. This means that being called to the work of spiritual guidance is one of the greatest of blessings. What work is greater than healing the heart, rebuilding the divine temple that houses our soul? Our heart of hearts holds that which is most valuable in us and most deeply valuable in the world. And we are additionally blessed that helping to heal the hearts of others also heals our own hearts.

 References

Fadiman, J. and Frager, R. *Essential Sufism*. San Francisco: HarperCollins, 1997.

TRANSPERSONAL PSYCHOLOGY
AND SPIRITUAL DIRECTION

In the following discussion we explore the interface between psychology and spiritual guidance. All three essays are written by authors who are both clinical psychologists and gifted spiritual guides. They reflect on the fundamental principles of spiritual guidance from a sophisticated psychological perspective.

Paul Roy discusses four basic principles in spiritual guidance—mindfulness, discernment, compassion, and appreciation of differences. Mindfulness includes both awareness and presence, an essential element in guidance. Discernment is at the heart of the guidance process. It means to notice the movements or stirrings within ourselves, and to decide how to respond to these movements. The third principle is compassion, a basic ingredient in all our relationships. Finally, appreciation of differences includes the first three principles. It means to attend to the present moment in a discerning way to awaken compassion. In appreciating our differences we are also called to remember that we are all living one life, inextricably bound together with each other and with all life.

Gerry Hair reflects on his thirty years of experience in guidance. He stresses the importance of working with three basic questions in guidance: "Who is the holy? Where is the holy? What is the relationship?" Gerry argues that we are always working with these questions in guidance, but too often we ask these questions unconsciously. He asks us to consider how we can hold these questions when working with others who are in pain and struggling before God.

Sean O'Laoire discusses the importance of story in our spiritual development. He suggests we move from the chaos of "before story" to the development of story, and then beyond the limits of our stories. Sean writes that storytelling has always been the greatest tool in therapy and in all kinds of spiritual guidance. Human history begins with the era of before story, when there were no myths, no cosmologies, no conception of God. With Cro-Magnons we find in the cave paintings evidence of the beginnings of cosmology, myth and story. About five hundred thousand-years-ago, as a species, we entered Storytelling Time and began to listen to and create story. Sean suggests there are four different kinds of stories. First is the *event story*, designed to interpret or explain certain events in our lives. Second is *personal mythology*, made up of a string of event stories, which provides us with a sense of personal identity. Third is *history*, the mythology that binds together a tribe or community. Fourth is *cosmology,* where as a culture we create a story to make sense of our place in the universe. Unfortunately, our personal and cultural stories tend to separate us, even to lead us to crucify each other. In guidance we can encourage our guidees to let go of their attachments to their personal stories and myths, to go beyond what separates us, and to realize we are all incarnations of God having diverse human experiences. Sean reminds us, "We are not separate from each other, and we are not separate from God."

Four Principles in Spiritual Guidance

When we talk about spiritual guidance, there are probably $n+1$ definitions, n being the number of people asked to define it. I'm not going to try to define spiritual guidance. There are probably equally as many definitions of spirituality, and I'm not going to try to define spirituality. There are certainly many definitions of transpersonal psychology, so I'm not going to go there either.

What I'd like to do instead is to operationalize both transpersonal psychology and spiritual guidance in the way that I currently understand them. This operationalizing is something that comes from the kind of education that we strive to impart at the Institute of Transpersonal Psychology.

Several years ago, the faculty at the Institute got together and we asked ourselves, "What is it we'd like our students to leave ITP with? What is it we'd like them to take away from their education that will make a difference in the world?" After having eliminated intellectual knowledge, because we know that they will already take that away to some degree, we came up with four values that we have tried to allow to inform everything we do at ITP. Those four values are: mindfulness, discernment, compassion, and appreciation of differences. Encouraging these values is what I believe spiritual guidance to be.

Mindfulness

The first value is mindfulness. I understand mindfulness to be primarily a quality of presence. I would define presence both in terms of attending to what is and also as being in the present moment. I see spiritual guidance as a process in which a guide accompanies another person with a view to developing and attending to what is present and what is in the present moment. Both the guide and the one being guided have the challenge and responsibility to attend to what is and to be in the present moment.

This means being able to focus and ask of yourself: What do you notice? What are you aware of? When I learned hypnotherapy, I learned to ask, "Are you aware of your tongue in your mouth?" The answer was no, I wasn't. "Are you aware of your foot on the floor?" Well, not really, no. "Are you aware of the people in this room? Are you aware that the present is not just here? Are you aware that in the present moment you are (or can be) present to the relief workers in Southeast Asia? Are you aware that in the present moment, you are a part of what is going on in Iraq? Are you aware that in the present moment, a parent is hugging a child?"

Developing this kind of mindfulness is at the core of spiritual guidance whether you are the guide or the one being guided. Just the other day, I heard somebody teaching about Sufism, and she was making the distinction between guru and disciple in some traditions, and teacher and student (in Arabic, *murshid* and *murid*) in Sufism. The guru will send the disciple to climb the mountain, to see what they can see and learn what they can learn from climbing the mountain. The *murshid* will say, "Let us climb the mountain together." It seems to me that climbing the mountain together is part of the essence of spiritual guidance. We come there together. We climb the mountain together. We seek to be present together.

St. Catherine of Siena once said, "Wisdom is so kind and wise that wherever you may look, you can learn something about God."[8] Practicing mindfulness can help us find the Divine in every aspect of our lives. It is surely a major aspect of the work of spiritual guidance.

Discernment

In my opinion, the second value is at the very core of the spiritual guidance process, namely discernment. I would define the process of discernment in this way: if I attend to the present moment within myself and around me, do I experience movements or stirrings within me? Can I tap into that place within me that understands or sees the origins of those movements? Can I then decide to respond or not to respond to those movements? Can I distinguish between the various movements to make decisions about response to each individually?

If we are to live in this world with a deepened sense of spirit, if we are to tap into the best that lives within each of us, if we are to walk this earth in a way that contributes to the life of the world, then we must attend to what moves us and figure out what it is that we are to respond to and how it is that we are to respond.

For example, I can think about the call to be a spiritual guide. What is it that moves me to be a spiritual guide? What feelings come with that movement? How is that movement inspired? If I am not in the present moment as I test this movement, I must come back to the present moment.

Frederick Buechner suggests, in *Wishful Thinking: A Theological ABC,* that vocation is where your deep gladness meets the world's deep hunger. When I am in the present moment, I must consider whether I am able to touch both the inner gladness and the world's hunger.

Spiritual guidance must bring people to that intersection of inner stirring and the great needs of our world. Only in this way does spirituality develop in a truly authentic way.

Compassion

The third aspect of spiritual guidance that I would like to focus on is compassion. I'm a psychotherapist. I do a lot of couple therapy. Especially in that work, I have noticed that the first casualty in conflict is compassion. People forget to tap into each other, to understand each other, to experience each other through compassion. The death of compassion is the death of our ability to understand the suffering of another. It is the death of our ability to be willing to identify with the suffering of another. It is the death of our creativity in attending to the suffering of another. When we lose compassion, the other becomes expendable and incidental to our existence or to our well-being. I see the development of compassion as a natural outgrowth of our willingness to attend to the present in a discerning way.

Here is an exercise to practice. Come to the present moment, and consider these questions: What stirs in you as you feel the suffering of the world? As you think about the suffering of someone near to you? What is it that calls for compassionate response in your life?

The Dalai Lama writes, "The qualities of love and compassion are utterly fundamental for finding happiness. I consider compassion to be the basis and supreme support of human kind. This eminent quality that induces us to love our neighbor, to come to his aid when he is suffering, and to forget ourselves for his sake is one that only human beings are capable of awakening, and whenever they do so, they are the first to derive happiness from it."

Appreciation of Differences

Finally, appreciation of differences requires that we attend to the present moment in a discerning way to awaken compassion in us, not just or even primarily for ourselves, but for those around us. All of this has to be in the service of realizing that we are all really living one life, that we are sharing one planet, that we are inextricably connected to one another. Each of us is unique, and each of us is part of everyone else.

I encourage all spiritual guides to think of those in your life whom you perceive to be different from you. See if you put anybody in boxes or cages or categories or pigeon-holes. Think of the world and how we capitalize on difference.

In conclusion, Anthony de Mello says this about true spirituality, "The students asked the master, "What is spirituality?" He said, "Spirituality is that which succeeds in bringing one to inner transformation." The students then asked, "But if I apply the traditional methods handed down by the masters, is that not spirituality?"

The master answered, "It is not spirituality if it does not perform its function for you. A blanket is no longer a blanket if it does not keep you warm, so spirituality does change. People change. Needs change. What was spirituality once is spirituality no more. What generally goes under the name of spirituality is merely the record of past methods." To which de Mello adds, "Don't cut the person to fit the coat."

Those four values of mindfulness, discernment, compassion, and appreciation of differences, I believe, form the core of what we do as spiritual guides. The values provide spiritual guides a common set of reference points because they are applicable across religious traditions, across spiritual traditions, across wisdom traditions, across political traditions. They enable us to be present to a world that really needs the work that we do.

References

Buechner, Frederick. *Wishful Thinking: A Theological ABC*. San Francisco: HarperCollins, 1973.

de Mello, Anthony, S.J. *The Song of the Bird*. New York: Doubleday, 1984.

Hafiz. *The Gift: Poems by Hafiz*. Ladinsky, Daniel J., trans. New York: Viking Penguin, 1999.

His Holiness the Dalai Lama. *The Spirit of Peace: Teachings on Love, Compassion, and Everyday Life*. London: Thorsons, 2002.

Ladinsky, Daniel J. *Love Poems from God: Twelve Sacred Voices from the East and West*. New York: Viking Penguin, 2002.

Whyte, David. *The House of Belonging*. Langley, WA: Many Rivers Press, 1996.

Three Basic Questions for the Spiritual Guide

About thirty years ago, I was part of a group of young Jesuits at the Jesuit Renewal Center in Milford, Ohio. We had been doing spiritual direction for a while, and decided that we could share our skills. More people were coming than we could witness in spiritual direction so we decided to start a training program. One of my colleagues checked around and found there were three spiritual direction training programs in the country. That was 1975. This same colleague checked again about five years ago. He found more than one hundred spiritual direction training programs in this country, and I'm sure it has kept growing.

What is that saying to us about who we are and what we're doing? It means that in spite of, or maybe because of, all the terrible suffering that the culture is having, there is an awakening occurring. There is a hunger that is manifesting itself spiritually in our friends, our associates, our colleagues, and our families. They want to come and talk to someone who can hold them present to this sacred unfolding that is taking place.

When I think about the struggles of the church, especially in my own Roman Catholic tradition, or when I think of what we have been through with the past election, it is difficult to hold it all with an open heart and in balance because it is so dark and painful. But immediately, when I do something like go to a conference of spiritual leaders, I find my heart lifted and filled with hope. I'm reminded that we are building an incredible community.

66

With my peers, I have found myself saying, "Gerry, you are in the presence of realized holiness." Every person who walks into our life is holiness, but it may not be so realized. That is our work, as spiritual guides. We stand and hold people so that we're there to midwife the next unfolding that they need in their lives. We are there to serve.

After thirty years of a full-time job listening to people and offering spiritual direction in groups, giving spiritual conferences, trainings, and so forth, I would like to share some elements that I find are the grounding of what I am trying to do. I don't think this will be a taxing list in any way. It is just the basics. In fact, I have narrowed it down to one question. The question that I think we always have to hold is, "What am I doing?"

"What am I doing?" is the most important question because if you and I think our shadow is not interfering with the way we're doing spiritual direction or spiritual guidance, we're kidding ourselves. "What am I doing?" shows my willingness to keep questioning myself. "What am I doing?" has an essential component to it that is always continuing the process of allowing myself to be supervised by others' eyes.

If we're going to continue any kind of practice, therapy or spiritual direction, we must continue to take it to supervisory groups. The purpose of that is to keep looking at the shadow piece that can appear and take us into some place that is not useful for the person sitting with us. The shadow piece is very useful to us, though. If we work alone for too long we can get stuck in a loop. If we allow others to interact with what we do, we may find the shadow in places we didn't know to look. What a precious gift that is.

If we, as spiritual guides, are asking "What am I doing?" then I find there are also three major questions that every person who comes to us for guidance is asking. At times, people may ask these questions very directly and clearly; they can be straightforward, fully conscious. Often enough, though, these three questions are being asked unconsciously. The first question is "Who is the Holy?" The second question is "Where is the Holy?" The third question is "What is our relationship?" Those questions will repeat themselves over and over again. As a spiritual guide, I'm always listening for the way those questions are manifesting themselves. It may be in symbol. It may be in image. It may be in a dream. It may be in a story. There are a thousand ways the Holy is manifesting itself, but these three questions are a guide for me to stay present to whoever is before me.

For example, I recognize these questions in a person saying, "Geez, I don't know what I'm doing. My religion and I are having a hard time. I'm just not working this thing out right," and so forth. I hear them asking: Who is the Holy? And how is it manifesting in this religion? Where is it in this religion? Where is it in my life? Those questions then become the resource for moving to the next layer of whatever this person needs to know.

What is interesting is that you ask the question as a beginner in the spiritual life, and then the question changes. It's a moving question. It shifts, and you wake up. One day you realize simply: God is out there. But that is just the beginning. You may go through many understandings before you bring God from "out there" in closer. Eventually you wake up again: there's no you. There's no me. There's no separation. There's no "I" that the mystics hold to us with an utterly pure mirror. As a spiritual guide, my work is to keep waking up to where I am in my own spiritual journey, but also to know that this question is going to move and be changing in the people I walk with through the whole process of spiritual direction.

About twenty-five years ago, I found myself asking about how to understand these stages of development. This is where transpersonal spirituality and psychology comes into play. I was aware that Maslow had done work understanding the stages of development in psychology. Fowler had done it with faith. Kohlberg had done it with morality. There had been wonderful insights about stages of spiritual development that have come from the tradition of mystics. But it wasn't enough. Along came Ken Wilber who took spirituality from North, South, East, and West, and found stages of spiritual development analogous to what the other developmental people did in their fields. He actually began to name some of the features that are part of each stage of spiritual development, all the way to the non-dual mystic. It was a stunning achievement. I don't think that everyone has to buy Wilber's ideas. Wilber is not easy to read. After the first time you have cracked your head on it, you go back and read it again, and you realize you have missed some fundamental piece. We need someone to do a kind of translating that makes Wilber available to those of us on the ground doing the everyday work. That someone is us. It is our job to translate Wilber's arcane, unapproachable language and make it available. We've been given an extraordinary, exquisite gift if we pay attention to the stages of spiritual development that Wilber has given us.

We have been given a framework at last for understanding spiritual direction and spiritual development. Wilber was able to read mountains of material from so many traditions, synthesize it, and find stages of development that paralleled across them. We have his work as a valuable tool to help us as we hold people in the process of spiritual direction.

One point Wilber can make for us is that every tradition can offer something to guide us. One grounding in this spiritual life that came to me out of the Jesuits, out of St. Ignatius of Loyola, was a way to prepare for the spiritual exercise of prayer. St. Ignatius had a little phrase he would say before you started. He said, "As I prepare for the mediation, I will check in with my heart's desire." That didn't mean a lot to me at the time. It just went through me; I didn't quite get it. As time has gone on, though, the notion of heart's desire has been a profound touchstone for my work as a spiritual director.

I find that when people are in touch with their heart's desire, there are two features present. One is that they are at home inside themselves spiritually in some sense. I do not mean they have worked out all of their psychological, social, political, or spiritual issues. I mean that at another level they are at home in themselves. The second feature is that they have a direction. The direction is not a perfectly laid out ten-year plan. The direction sounds more like: "I know spirit is unfolding in me. I'm in touch with that. It's taking me." I have found that with individuals and groups, we can stay on track if we stay tuned to the question of the heart's desire. When people lose themselves and get away from their heart's desire, they are discombobulated and lost. Their lives are being taken over by whatever the "stuff" is that impinges on them all the time.

If someone comes to spiritual guidance feeling that they don't know what their heart's desire is, that is fine. They are still asking the question. I encourage people to hold the question. Walk with it. Walk with it like a koan: "What is my heart's deepest desire?" The holiness cannot *not* respond to you. It is completely impossible for it to be aloof. There is nothing in the Holy that is not being revealed 100 percent right now. Our task is getting through the filters to be able to listen to our heart's deepest desire. Whenever any of us gets lost, or gets lost with a client, we can come back to that question and ask it. No one will answer "my heart's desire is a Ferrari." The answer will be on a deeper level, and you will come immediately into the grounding of who a person is. It is a compass for the spiritual life, and it is also a home. It is very simple because it's fully 100 percent present everywhere, at every time, except for when we cover it up. It is sometimes easy to connect with it. It is sometimes not. It is sometimes difficult to sustain. That's just the way it is.

When faced with difficulty discovering your heart's desire, it can be easy to get lost and frustrated. I never thought that Thomas Aquinas would be coming back in my life, but I will turn to him now. Thomas Aquinas said there are four transcendentals. I will be very simple with it here. Whenever anyone is in touch with the One, the good, the true, and the beautiful, they are immediately awake in the Holy presence. When one of the transcendentals is present, all of them are present. Peter Berger added to this system and wrote that there is a fifth transcendental. It is humor. Whenever you are laughing, your mind stops. Remember the editor of *Saturday Review*, who was dying of cancer. He didn't know what to do. He tried everything. Finally, he started watching funny movies. What happened to him? He got a long, long remission from his cancer. He opened to the transcendental of humor. When people are stuck in other areas, humor is a place where the doors can open. You can see through, and then they can see through.

I have suggested many questions to hold as a spiritual guide. There is another, fundamental one I should address: what is the art of spiritual guidance? A friend of mine wrote a paper years ago called "From Swami to Guru in Spiritual Guidance." He said that ultimately what the guru is to be is a place for someone to come and sit down and be present to whatever is true in their life. The guru is not trying to figure out their enneagram point, their Myers-Briggs type, or what stage of spiritual development they are in. The guru is present to what this person is. Then that person wakes up to who they are because a spiritual guide is the mirror to who they are. A number of years ago it came to me that in the Christian tradition we would say, "They are to look in my eyes as a spiritual guide and see that they are the Christ. They are the holiness. They are the truth." Then the thought came to me, "Who do you think you are?" The answer is that I am nobody, because I look in their eyes and see that I am the truth. I am the holiness. I am the life. Here we sit in this holiness together. Julian of Norwich says it well: "We are 'oned' to God, unchangeable goodness. Therefore between God and my soul, there is neither wrath nor forgiveness because there is no between."

I will return now to the three original questions: who is God, where is God, and what is my relationship? Spiritualities rise and fall on the way they answer these questions. How do we accompany people to hold those questions, when they are in terrible pain and struggling before God? I will answer with a story from my own life.

It was 1972. I had a cousin with leukemia. It was a fatal leukemia. She was sixteen years old, one of ten children. I was supposed to be the one with spiritual awakening because I was a Jesuit studying spirituality.

But I was the one in the family who was enraged. I was so pissed off that she was going to die, I spent the year raging. It was all I could do, just rage to God. I was sitting down studying toward the end of the year. It was in May. I wouldn't use the same language now, but for me at that particular stage, this awareness came: "I sent my son to surrender to all this suffering to awaken you, my beloved. Would you do that with your child?"

Now I have a different understanding of theology, and I receive awareness differently. But that was the language I could receive at that particular stage. I began weeping. I wept for an hour. At the end of the hour, somebody called and said, "Mary Pat just died. She died about an hour ago."

If you are lucky, pain and loss will crack you open and help you receive awareness. They are the places where your spirituality rises and falls, and where you are invited to meet the holiness on a level far beyond the way you were ever able to do in your life before. It is a gift, but a terrible gift. Our work is to offer presence to people in all stages of development, in all stages of questioning, in all stages of receiving these spiritual gifts. We are most able to offer this presence if we are also asking the important questions of ourselves.

Spiritual Guidance and Story

The wisest creature on planet earth, according to Irish mythology, was a salmon. Not just any salmon, but a very specific salmon that we call Fintan. Fintan lived in a lake over which grew a very special hazel tree that dropped nuts; we call them the "nuts of knowledge." Fintan ate the nuts and acquired wisdom. He was thousands of years old. The belief was that whoever captured and ate the fish would acquire all its knowledge and all its wisdom.

Generations and generations of Irish fishermen attempted to capture him and failed miserably. Finally the philosophers joined in the search. One philosopher devoted his entire life to trying to catch Fintan. He camped out by the lake for forty years. For forty years, this philosopher devised various strategies to capture Fintan and never succeeded.

Then one day, Fintan, it seems, just gave himself up. The philosopher captured him, was totally elated, built a fire, put him on a spit, and began to cook him. Just then, a little boy wandered by. This little boy was a child called Fionn Mac Cumhail (a very famous Irish character). Fionn was about nine years old at the time.

The philosopher said, "I want you to watch over this fish. It's going to be cooking for the next three hours. I'm really tired. I need to take a nap, but under no circumstances are you to taste this fish." So Fionn agreed, and the philosopher lay down and started to sleep. After about half an hour, as the young boy was watching the salmon cook, a blister came up on the skin because the fire was so hot. He reached out his thumb to touch it, and he burst the blister. It hurt like hell so he stuck his thumb in his mouth, and he sucked on it. A few moments later, the philosopher woke up. He took one look at the boy and said, "You ate it didn't you?" The boy said, "No, I didn't eat it. Look, it's still there." But the philosopher said, "I can see it in your face. I can see it in your eyes. You've totally changed. You may as well take the rest of it now and eat it because it's no good to me."

And from that day onward, Fionn Mac Cumhail, whenever he needed to prognosticate, would stick his thumb in his mouth. We've a special name for this finger in Irish. It's called *méar feasa*, which means the "finger of wisdom." We also have a name for the index finger, it's called *méar an eolais*, which means the "finger of knowledge." The thumb and index fingers are very different. The index is just for giving directions. But the thumb represents true wisdom. So, the story goes, when you see your baby suck on its thumb, it's prognosticating. It's in touch with its own wisdom.

I was raised by my grandfather on these kinds of wisdom stories from the Irish tradition for the first ten years of my life. Then, at age twenty-six, I went to Africa and spent fourteen years living in Kenya with the wisdom traditions of the Kalenjin people. I have a great love for stories. Recently, though, I have run into a problem. I have begun trying to create a theory of human evolution, and the theory is telling me that stories are finished. In order to make this understandable, I will need to tell the story of storytelling. I will entitle it: "From Babyhood to Buddhahood and from Chaos to Christ-Consciousness." Why tell the story of storytelling? Because storytelling has been the greatest tool and the greatest resource for therapy and spiritual direction of all kinds.

I want to suggest that there are three phases to human evolution. This is a very simplistic model. I call these phases BST, DST, and AST: *Before Story Time*, *During Story Time*, and *After Story Time*.

There's a truism that would have us believe that ontology recapitulates phylogeny. In other words, the evolution of an individual in society reenacts the entire history of the whole species. There is some truth in this. I have a belief that somewhere over the last few million years, as we evolved from the animal kingdom, for a long period of time, particularly as we were developing the use of language, there were no stories. We lived life through instinct, and it was a very scary place to be. Life was totally uncontrollable, utterly unpredictable, and from moment to moment, there were no ways of recognizing patterns. We didn't have stories or precedents. There were no guides as yet. There were no rhythms that we could discern. So we reacted to various situations instinctively and in the moment. There was no way of learning from these situations.

At this stage, there was no science. There were no explanations. There were no cosmologies. There was no mythology. There was no need for God. This stage perhaps lasted up to fifty thousand years ago. With the evolution of Cro-Magnon Man, we get the first evidence of cave paintings and the possibility of religion, stories, cosmologies, and mythologies.

This first era in human evolution was very frightening, I imagine. It must have been very, very difficult to not have a grandfather to prepare us for what we were going to experience in life. As with the species, so also with the individual: little children experience the same thing until they can form images. Finally around fifteen months, we begin to develop language skills so we can manipulate symbols and thus we can be told stories and we can retain stories. So the first era of human evolution, it seems to me, is *Before Story Time* when no explanations are possible, no science is possible, and there is no need for a God.

About fifty thousand years ago as a species and around age fifteen months as individual children, we come into *Story Time*. Then something different happens. We learn to listen to and create stories.

I suggest that we create four kinds of stories. The first ones I call *Event Stories*. Particular things happen in our lives, and we create stories to interpret them or explain them to ourselves. That is the first level of story telling.

The second level of storytelling is what I would call *Personal Mythology*. I string together a whole bunch of *Event Stories* in my life. From these, I fashion my sense of personal identity. It defines who I think I am. My *Personal Mythology* is the sum total of the *Event Stories* of my life.

The third level of storytelling, I believe, is *History*, where as a tribe or as a community or as a culture, we create a myth that binds us all together. This is the sum total of the individual *Personal Mythologies* of the group that constitute the tribe or the culture. Finally, the fourth level, the highest level of all, is *Cosmology*, where as an entire species, we create a story to tell of our place in the universe.

Initially, these stages allow us to make sense of our experiences. Initially, they allow us to bond as a tribe or as a community. Initially, they allow us to say what our place might be as a species in God's plan. But there are problems at every stage.

For instance, at the *Event Story* stage, the story I make up to explain an incident in my life can liberate me or it can crucify me. I currently have a client, a woman, who was mugged ten years ago. She came to see me fairly recently. She is a very petite woman, and she said, "I'm just a little woman. I'm very fragile. I'm very vulnerable. Life sucks. I can't trust men. I can't go out of doors." I said, "When did it happen?" She answered, "Ten years ago." I asked, "How long did the mugging last?" She replied, "About three minutes."

A three-minute event that happened a decade ago has continued to crucify this woman for ten years. Now, in fact, it is not the incident that crucifies her, it is the story she has made up around the incident. We all do this constantly. The stories we tell ourselves about the incidents of our lives can either liberate us or they can crucify us. Mainly, in my experience as a clinical psychologist, we tend to make up stories that crucify us.

The second level of story is the *Personal Myth*. The *Personal Myth* is a way of self-identification where we typically take a nonrepresentative sample of the billions of experiences we've had as a human being, stitch them together, and create an identity out of them. Imagine someone sits beside you in a plane and says, "What's your name? Who are you?" and you tell them a whole bunch of incidents that happened to you. As far as you're concerned, that explains who you are. That group of incidents make up your sense of identity. We act as if we are the sum total of the *Event Stories* that we've made up. This can allow us to feel victimized by life.

In the third stage, *History*, we make up a story as a culture, and the story gives us cohesion as a group. That's the good news. The bad news is that we then use this strength to bludgeon other cultures. It is the story of our cultural history as a nation that allows us to go into Iraq and kill a hundred thousand people and justify it, feel like we're liberating them, and say that we are on a crusade of "*infinite justice.*" Every culture does it. These are the problems in cultural stories: they are the histories that bludgeon the opposition and create prejudice. Once again, our sense of self, as a culture, is based on a nonrepresentative sample of our experiences as a nation.

There was an interesting test done with English and French school kids a few years ago. They were asked to name the thirty most important battles fought between England and France. The kids came up with lists, and they were all real battles. But there was one big problem: there was almost no overlap between the lists that the French kids came up with and the lists that the English kids came up with. The French kids could only remember, because they had only been taught, the glorious battles in which France had won. The English kids could only remember, because they had only been taught, the great battles in which England had won. This is an example of how our histories are never representative of our experiences. They are based on a very biased sample.

The most important of all our stories, and thus the most important problems we face, are in our *Cosmologies*. The cosmologies are the stories we have made up as a species to explain our place in the world and beyond. Our first fallacy here is that we think "ours" is the only cosmos that exists, but quantum mechanics tells us that there are ten to the power of twenty-seven brand new universes created every second per cubic centimeter of eleven dimensional mathematical space. That's a lot of cosmoses. Most of those are mathematical duds, but even if the tiniest percentage of them survive, it's a staggering number. It is so foolish of us to pretend that this is the only cosmos.

Almost nobody knows what the second-most important equation of the twentieth century is. We can all spit out $E = MC^2$, but by consensus of the scientific community, the second most important formula of the twentieth century says the following: "$N = N^* \times F_p \times F_e \times F_l \times F_i \times F_c \times L$," is attributed to a man named Frank Drake who was a radio astronomer in the 1950s. It is a probability estimate of the number of civilizations, just in the Milky Way galaxy alone, capable of developing technology that would enable them to communicate with other beings outside of their own solar system. A conservative estimate of the number of such civilizations is about two million. The Milky Way galaxy is only one of about one hundred fifty billion galaxies in this known universe, which is only one of the ten to the power of twenty-seven universes, generated every second per cubic centimeter of eleven dimensional mathematical space. But in our "common sense cosmology," we act as if this is the only cosmos. Then, we act as if we are the most evolved species within this cosmos.

What do we do with these cosmologies? Not only do they divide us from all sentient life forms on the planet, but they even divide us from each other, religion to religion. I believe that Jesus Christ and the Buddha and the other great avatars weren't sent as teachers among us. They were sent as prototypes of where human evolution is meant to be headed. But inevitably, when a great charismatic figure comes among us, here's what happens: We kill the prophet. We eviscerate the teaching. We sanitize what's left. We interpret it literally. We enforce it dogmatically. Then we kill those who won't believe the sanitized version. First we kill the prophet; then we kill the teaching; and finally, we kill the unbelievers who won't believe the sanitized version of the teaching. That is what happens when cosmology goes wrong, when the great story goes wrong.

So what is the way forward? Thomas Aquinas and the great scholastics teach us that grace builds upon nature. In other words, spirituality builds upon psychology. The further reaches of human evolution are built upon our psychotherapeutic interventions at an earlier stage. It is a seamless garment. To divide psychotherapy from spirituality doesn't make any sense. To divide psychotherapy from spiritual direction doesn't make any sense. We're dealing with the same spirit in its evolutionary trajectory.

Where do we need to proceed, as clinicians or as spiritual guides? There are some people who are still stuck in the BST, or *Before Story Time*. For them, life is totally chaotic. As spiritual guides and as clinicians, we must bring them into *During Story Time*. They have to have a story. Until they have a story, life is totally unpredictable.

But that is not the end of the journey. Once you get to *During Story Time*, it is easy to get stuck. Most of us are stuck in *During Story Time*. Only a very few have gone to *After Story Time*. For most of us stuck in *During Story Time*, we are being crucified by the *Event Stories* or we're being held back by the *Personal Mythology*. As a nation, we're being crucified by our cultural stories. As a species, we're being crucified by our cosmologies. Therefore it seems to me that the purpose of great psychotherapy and the purpose of great spiritual direction is to invite those who already have stories to begin telling *better* stories: to let go of the stories that divide, to let go of the personal *Event Stories* that crucify us, to let go of the personal identities based on nonrepresentative samples, to let go of the histories, the cultural stories that allow us to crucify other nations. We have to be offering people the possibility of better stories so ultimately they can move to where there are no stories anymore. That place, where the stories end, is the third stage.

Carl Jung once said that in order to do any useful psychotherapy with somebody, you've first got to join them where they're at, and then move them from where they are to where they want to be or could be. Eventually, I want to bring my clients to the following: life as we experience it is just a temporary incarnational dip.

I wrote a book a few years ago that I entitled *Spirits in Spacesuits*. I chose that title because it represents to me that basically we are spirit beings. We are bite-sized bits of God choosing to have a human experience. In order to have a human experience, we have to put on a "spacesuit." The spacesuit has four qualities: it has physicality; it has emotionality; it has intellectuality; and it has personality. But these are attributes of the spacesuit. They're not attributes of the essence of the Spirit within the spacesuit.

Therefore I believe we travel as cohort groups of souls from lifetime to lifetime. In spite of being a Catholic priest, I am a total heretic because I subscribe to the theory of reincarnation. It makes eminent psychological and mystical and theological sense to me that we dip in and out of our incarnation as a part of our learning process. The incarnation may be on a planet such as Earth or it may be on one of the other two million planets in this galaxy capable of developing life forms that can communicate with those outside their own solar system. We may choose an incarnation on a planet that has no emotional possibility but has extraordinary intellectual possibility.

I believe that as souls we make a choice to experience our spiritual evolution in many different kinds of environments. There is nobody on the planet now who didn't at some stage put their hand up and say, "Send me," or "I volunteer to go here." Our purpose in any incarnation is not to learn anything. It is not to discover anything. It is merely to remember who we are, where we've come from, what we've come to do, and what our ultimate destiny is.

The Jewish Talmudic tradition says that just before we're born, the angel of night, who is called Aiyella, pinches our nostrils and presses on our upper lip (that's why you've got indentations in both places) in order to create amnesia for whom we are and what we've come to do.

There is an African tribe in which the elders sequester each pregnant woman, typically about seven months into her confinement. They put her in a hypnotic trance and speak to the baby. They believe that the mother's voice will be used by the child to answer questions. They ask two questions of the child: "What is your name?" and "What are you coming to do?" Whatever name the child speaks, that is the name the tribe will give it. Whatever mission the child identifies, that is the mission the entire group will try to support.

There is no happenstance or coincidence or accident about us all being here. We chose our planet, a ball of fire with a little crust over the top, subject to the vicissitude of Gaia. We chose a planet subject to the awakening of and the movements of tectonic plates and the evolution of life forms here. All of us have done that consciously.

But we've all forgotten why we've come, and we've forgotten that we've come as a group. We're almost like the 49ers in the Super Bowl. We create this extraordinary game plan before the game begins. Then we go out into the field, and everybody wants to be Joe Montana. There were some who came down here and took extremely difficult birth places and birth circumstances on the understanding that those more privileged among us would be there for them. We came as a team, all 6.5 billion of us. Sometimes people accept less than ideal circumstance in order to offer the rest of us the opportunity to exercise compassion or to develop scientific abilities to predict earthquakes or to cure illnesses, but we're all in it as a team.

John Donne said, "No man is an island . . . Ask not for whom the bell tolls, it tolls for thee." What is the mission for those of us who remain behind? It seems to me that it is to wake up to who we are and why we've come, and to let go, finally, of the illusion of separate identity. We are not separate from each other, and we are not separate from God.

The evolution of therapy and the evolution of spiritual guidance call us to bring those who have no stories whatsoever into *During Storytelling Time*, to bring those who are stuck with stories that crucify them into better stories that heal them, and, finally, to call those with "good stories" to move into *After Storytime*. At this stage, once again, there are no gods. At this stage, once again, there are no explanations necessary. At this stage, once again, there is no science. At this stage, once again, there is no learning, and at this stage, once again, there is no discovery. There is only remembering. We are now in contact with our true face. That is the journey of the therapist and the spiritual guide: to move us through these stages until once more we come back to a place where there is no need for gods, for explanations, for *Event Stories*, for *Personal Mythologies*, for *Histories*, or for *Cosmologies*.

At the third stage, the only necessary use of stories is perhaps to integrate the little ones, the babies who are being born and who need the training wheels of stories in order to prepare for the spiritual safari that takes them *After Story Time* again. The truly awakened person doesn't need a story anymore except to relate to people who need stories, or to relate to those who are beginning the journey for the first time. At that stage, when we have let go even of the great story, having moved from no story to bad stories to good stories to no stories once more, we can say, "If you meet the Buddha on the road, kill him." Or with Meister Eckhart, you can cry, "I pray daily to God to rid me of God."

THE MYSTICS AND
SPIRITUAL DIRECTION

This third section discusses spiritual guidance and the wisdom of the mystics. Rob Hopcke, a Jungian psychotherapist and spiritual guide, reflects on the dark night of the soul as discussed in the writings of John of the Cross. He points out that most people misunderstand the dark night as simply dryness and desolation. In fact, it refers to coming closer to God in silence, God's silence and our own. In a culture that is filled with television and background music, we need to learn to become comfortable with silence.

James Neafsey shares a poetic creation story that emerged in him during am eight-day silent retreat. In this story, God's spinning top generates the universe. The spinning top also represents our deep self, which connects us to God, to each other, and to all creation. Jim reminds us that the work of spiritual guidance is to support the joy, life, love, and spiritual yearning in those who come to us.

Spiritual Direction and Mystical Experience

When contemplating the relationship between mystical experience and spiritual direction, as a Jungian psychotherapist in Berkeley and a practicing Roman Catholic spiritual director, I realize that my companionship and presence with God is one that has come to me primarily through silence. Whether it is my work of psychological healing with my clients, my practice of spiritual companionship with my fellow parishioners, or even my more formal role as volunteer spiritual director at San Quentin State Prison, I cannot help but draw from the large and very deep Catholic-Christian tradition of spiritual direction by contemplative mystics, especially John of the Cross, Meister Eckhart, and St. Teresa.

Doing direction is very different from *writing about* spiritual direction, and I am aware here of having to fumble some toward a working definition of mysticism. How I tend to describe mysticism is first by noticing that so many of our experiences of the Divine come to us through mediated forms, for example, music, art, poetry, dancing. God comes through the medium of the created beauty of a poem or a song. By contrast, a mystical experience is often *im*-mediate, that is, direct and *un*-mediated, which is, relatively speaking, a rare thing for most of us, and thus sometimes difficult for people to recognize as a visitation from the Divine. So, engaging in contemplative or ascetic practices or certain kinds of prayers is not the mystical experience itself. Those practices are not even a guarantee of receiving the grace of such direct experience. Rather, they are intended to be the media of the unmediated, as it were, to open up a pathway to an immediate experience of the Divine in one's soul.

Because we live in a culture that does not truly value silence, I find myself as a director in a very unusual and privileged place with my directees. They so frequently enter direction in order to make a transition in their relationship with God. Having been engaged in contemplative practices and experiences of the Divine through the various media of ritual, liturgy, and prayers like the rosary, they have been finally granted the grace of a mystical experience of God in silence. When the bottom falls out of one's inner life and opens on to the vastness of the Divine in this way, there are very few places in this culture to go; there are very few places to sit in this silence, in this immediate, wordless speech of God.

Many of the concepts from the Christian mystics have been popularized and, in particular, I wish to address the "dark night of the soul"—what it is and how I believe it has been largely misunderstood. In the writings of St. John of the Cross, the "dark night of the soul" is what I just described: God's silence and our own — working as an entryway into an unmediated experience of the Divine. Most people, however, unfortunately think about "the dark night of the soul" as a period of spiritual dryness or desolation, a spiritual state to be avoided. In my experience, this negative view of the "dark night" is what most people do believe St. John to have meant. But it is not what he meant, nor do I think that it is either an accurate or a helpful way to move into the wondrous night that beckons us all into a fuller, more intimate experience of God. So much that sustains our lives and souls can only happen in the dark of night. The nighttime is a time of quiet and rest. It is a time when the food we have eaten gets digested and we are nourished. It's a time of listening. It's the time of dreams. It's the time when we pull back, reflect, and sit in the gentle glow of moonlight. The night is not to be avoided, but rather understood as simply a natural part of our cycle and our path. In fact, the night is to be sought out.

To flesh out the notions put forward by St. John, there is no such thing as "the dark night of the soul," per se, in his writings. He talks about many different "nights" throughout the spiritual journey. One is the "night of the senses," and what most people would probably call "the dark night of the soul" is actually what he would call the "night of the senses"—a direct, inexpressible experience of God beyond sense, beyond word, beyond description. This "night of the senses" can be disturbing for us and our ego, because we so clearly have no control over it and cannot really communicate to others about it. That is the reason why John called it "night": human powers are eclipsed by the brilliance of the Divine. However, in the midst of such human helplessness, I try to keep in mind that C. G. Jung once said every defeat for the ego is a victory for the Self, which is to say, for God.

I have gone through some very difficult times in the last year, and in my own spiritual direction, it has been very difficult to see where God is leading me. Throughout, in a very sensitive but uncompromising way, my director has continuously said, "Welcome to the night of the senses. You can't see forward. Rely on God."

John of the Cross likens this "night of the senses" to the early part of the evening. The sun has just set, so your sense impressions are still very real and alive. Yet as we move later and later on into the evening, soon our sense impressions will fade, at which point, he tells us, the next "night" begins, which he calls "the night of faith." Here we abandon ourselves and fall asleep in God, in faith that we will wake up. As lonely as it can be, this portion of the night, this "night of faith," can be a very restful and comforting place, just as secure as deep sleep can be. With faith, we realize we do not achieve our own salvation or wholeness. Rather, we come to know that we will be brought to wholeness, as long as we rest, remain calm, let go and let God.

The third night John then speaks of is "the night of God" in which ultimately, individual sense of self is extinguished, and we enter into direct union with God's will. That is the transition point I often see people coming into spiritual direction seeking some help with, for it represents a passage from performing specific contemplative practices to creating a more general contemplative way of life that reflects a resonance with the Divine everywhere and at all times, not just in a church or in prayer. This "night of God," is the most difficult spiritual state to describe. Creative expressions of beauty are about the only ways to really "speak" about it. One can only express the nature of this experience indirectly.

These various dark nights of the soul represent not a period of desolation or dryness, but the opposite, a beginning of the soul's true life and journey toward union with God. The night, of whatever form, is not something to be avoided and it's not something to be feared. Hence, at this particular time of rich growth, when people have a very counterintuitive experience of their contemplative practice falling by the wayside, and are encountering instead the direct, awesome silence of God, spiritual guidance plays a crucial role. At this point, we are called as spiritual guides to say to our companions, "Yes, that's exactly where you need to be going. Go into the silence, go into the night, go into the cloud of unknowing."

In editing Henri Nouwen's last book, *Sabbatical Journey*, a journal of his last year of life, I came across the following passage. In reading it, I immediately thought, "Shoot, if Henri Nouwen went through this, we should all take heart." He writes on September 3, 1995:

> Prayer is the bridge between my unconscious and conscious life. Prayer connects my mind with my heart, my will with my passion, my brain with my belly. Prayer is the way to let the life-giving spirit of God penetrate all the corners of my being. Prayer is the divine instrument of my wholeness, unity and peace. So what about my life of prayer? Do I like to pray? Do I want to pray? Do I spend time praying? Frankly, the answer is no to all three questions.
>
> "After 63 years of life and 38 years of priesthood, my prayer seems as dead as a rock. I remember my teenage years when I could hardly stay away from the church. For hours I would stay on my knees filled with a deep sense of Jesus's presence. I couldn't believe that not everyone wanted to pray. Prayer was

so intimate and so satisfying. It was during these prayer-filled years that my vocation to the priesthood was shaped. During the years that followed, I've paid much attention to prayer, reading about it, writing about it, visiting monasteries and houses of prayer and guiding many people on their spiritual journeys. By now, I should be full of spiritual fire consumed by prayer. Many people think I am. And they speak to me as if prayer is my greatest gift and deepest desire. The truth is that I do not feel much if anything when I pray. There are no warm emotions, bodily sensations or mental visions. None of my five senses is being touched. No special smells, no special sounds, no special sights, no special tastes and no special movements. Where as for a long time, the spirit acted so clearly through my flesh, now I feel nothing. I have lived with the expectation that prayer would come easier as I grow older and closer to death, but the opposite seems to be happening. The words darkness and dryness seem to best describe my prayer today. Are the darkness and the dryness of my prayer signs of God's absence or are they signs of a presence deeper and wider than my senses can contain? Is the death of my prayer the end of my intimacy with God or the beginning of a new communion beyond words, emotions and bodily sensations? As I sit down for half an hour to be in the presence of God and to pray, not much is happening to talk about to my friends. Still maybe this time is a way of dying with Jesus. The year ahead of me must be a year of prayer even though I say my prayers as dead as a rock. My prayer surely is, but not necessarily the spirit's prayer in me. Maybe the time has come to let go of my prayer, my effort to be close to God. My way of being in communion with the divine and to allow the spirit of God to blow freely in me.[9]

That is the essence of the dark night: we abandon our own individual sense of self, and we move into the silence willingly. With that desire, we open ourselves up fully to the action of the divine through us. After we surrender, the spirit bursts forth with certain truths of contemplative living. But in between the desire and the fruits, we are invited by God into the beautiful dark night.

 References

Nouwen, Henri, *Sabbatical Journey*. New York: Crossroad, 2001.

Breakthroughs in Spiritual Guidance

I am a spiritual director with roots in the Roman Catholic tradition. I received my formation as a spiritual guide in the tradition of St. Ignatius Loyola, a sixteenth-century Spanish mystic who founded the Jesuit Order. I originally intended to write an imaginary dialogue with St. Ignatius on the heart of spiritual guidance, and it might have been quite informative.

However, I have set a different task for myself. Jesus states that "Truly I tell you, whoever does not receive the kingdom of God as a little child will never enter it."[10] The imaginary conversation I intended to have with Ignatius would just be too serious, too removed from the direct experience of the energy of spiritual longing and the joy of its release. So instead of a serious dialogue with a recognized spiritual master, I will share a childlike creation story that emerged in poetic form during a silent retreat I made many years ago. It captures both the energy and joy that I believe are the very heart of spiritual guidance.

The context for writing the story was a silent, eight-day retreat. For the first six days of the retreat, anger, fear, anxiety, desire, and grief poured out in a steady stream during meditation and in my dreams at night. Then, on the seventh day of the retreat, there was a dramatic shift. During an afternoon meditation I felt the inner movement of my entire life from the present moment all the way back to my birth, where the movement seemed to encounter a wall or barrier. Suddenly, I seemed to be on the other side of that barrier in a vastness beyond time and space. The following creation story "wrote itself" over the next few hours.

Once upon eternity before there was a time or space,
A smile spread across God's face.
"Hallelujah!" cried God with glee,
"Let all creation come to be!"
That burst of joy created space,
A warm and loving playful place,
Ringing then and ever after
With the music of God's laughter.
Then God took a mighty jump—
"Up!" he called where his head bumped.
"Down!" he called where his feet thumped.
Next God stretched both arms out wide
Where each hand touched he made a side
And at the center, God placed a top
That's made to spin and never stop.
It whirled and twirled at such a pace,
That sparks flew out all over the place.
"My stars," said God with pure delight,
"How they shine with sparkling light!"
When the making of the stars was done,
God searched and found our shining sun.
He took a portion of its light
And squeezed it in his fist so tight
That when he opened up his hand,
Out popped the earth a ball of sand!
God spun the earth with all his might
To start the dance of dark and light
That we now know as day and night.
Then, just for fun,
God hurled the earth around the sun
And as earth circled far and near,
It passed through seasons of the year.
The seasons changed from cold to hot,
But rain and snow, well, God forgot.

The earth below got hard and dry
While up above just empty sky.
God then found a spot so cold
That when he breathed, or so I'm told,
Clouds puffed out and filled the air.
God wrapped them round the earth with care
Then clapped to make a thunder sound
And rain poured out upon the ground.
The earth was drenched by such a storm
That lakes and seas began to form.
Then God began to laugh and say,
"Wet sand and mud and squishy clay,"
"What a perfect place to play!"
God made mountain peaks on which to pray
And caves in which to hide away—
And where he dragged his toe,
Streams and rivers began to flow.
Then God had another notion,
To set the sea and air in motion.
He spun his top with such commotion
Waves rose and fell upon the ocean.
And where his spinning top would twirl,
Wind began to howl and swirl.
Then God made living things that grow.
Some grew tall.
Some grew low.
Some moved fast
Some moved slow.
Some soared above.
Some swam below.
Some liked it hot.
Some loved the snow.
But every creature that we know
Was made by God to be just so.

God had in mind just two more creatures,
Both equipped with special features.
He gave them legs on which to stand
And minds so they could understand.
Then God gave them this command,
"Eve and Adam now come to life,
I now pronounce you man and wife.
Love each other as I do
And love the things I made for you."
Then God made words so they could speak
And loving hearts so they could seek
What's good and true and right and free
The way God meant for us to be.
Each was the other's heart's delight
And both loved God with all their might
And when the day turned into night,
They hugged and held each other tight.
When God returned by light of day
He brought his top so they could play,
But first he had these words to say,
"Adam and Eve, you see this top?
It's made to spin and never stop.
It spins the stars you see at night.
It spins the sun which gives you light.
All through the year it sets the pace.
It keeps each season in its place.
It rocks the waves upon the ocean
And keeps the wind in constant motion.
In your hearts it glows with light
Showing you what's wrong and right.
When it spins things smoothly run
And all earth's creatures dwell as one.
So please be careful when you play
To spin the top in just this way.

Make sure it spins from left to right
And never let it out of sight
For if it spins the other way,
Everything will go astray.
Wind and water, earth and sun,
All living things that dwell as one
Will fall apart and come undone."
Then Eve and Adam understood
The meaning of both bad and good.
To spin along with God's own top
Brings joy and love that never stop.
To spin in any other way
Just brings trouble night and day.
So they spun the top from left to right,
And never left it out of sight
Until God took it home at night.
Then one dark and gloomy day,
They made a choice to disobey.
They formed their own top from some clay
And spun it quickly in reverse.
Things quickly went from bad to worse.
Creation had run with perfection
But now the top broke all connection.
Eve and Adam lost direction
And their hearts lost all affection.
Where love had been there now was fear.
The light inside became less clear.
When God returned next day to play,
He could hardly see the way.
There was hardly any light.
Everything was dark as night.
What had been straight was now all curvy.
The universe was topsy-turvy.
Then God saw the backwards top

And at once he shouted, "Stop!
Where did you get that crazy top?
What a mixed up mess you've made."
Adam and Eve were so afraid.
When God looked down and saw their fears,
He held them close and wiped their tears.
Then he whispered in their ears,
"What's done is done. Just let it be.
I'll find some way to set you free."
God tried and tried to set things right,
But Eve and Adam ran in fright
Whenever God came into sight.
So it was year after year,
They hid from God and lived in fear.
Finally God did find a way
To tell us what he had to say.
He hid his top in Baby Jesus
Knowing that would surely please us.
Jesus spoke of love and peace
And made the backward spinning cease.
Fear began to melt away
And in its place love came to stay.
When the final word was spoken,
On the cross his heart was broken.
Everyone was sad and cried,
They felt that God himself had died.
But when his tomb was opened wide
God's own top was found inside.
Knowing how we loved to play,
God left a gift for us that day
A spinning top in each one's heart
To spin out love and light the dark.
One other thing about that top,
It's made to spin and never stop

Until the day when all are free
To spin with God eternally.

This poem emerged in one afternoon with some revisions added over the years that followed. It was, for me, the release of a river of longing for God, which runs deeper than words or images. That is where the poem begins: "Once upon eternity before there was a time or space, / A smile spread across God's face." Before there were words, before time and space, there was the fertile void, the pregnant silence of eternity. When the silence becomes ripe for speech, the whole universe bursts forth as the laughter of God.

I want to touch on a few points where I see a connection between the poem and what the mystics teach us about spiritual guidance. The poem is expressed in playful, childlike images—but images that express core spiritual concepts. For example, the central image of the top represents what mystical traditions would call the heart, the center of the soul, the Divine Spark. Christians would call it the presence of the Holy Spirit within us.

In the Jewish tradition, Rabbi Nahman of Bratslav described this mystical center as a spinning top. "For in truth the entire universe is a spinning top which is called a *dreidel*. . . . All things in the world are part of this circular motion, reborn and transformed into one another. That which was above is lowered and that which was below is raised up. For in their root all of them are one."[11] For Rabbi Nahman the spinning dreidel expresses the creative play of opposites that manifests the dynamic underlying unity of creation.

In the Buddhist tradition the same reality is represented not by a top, but by the eight-spoked wheel of the dharma. At the center of the Tibetan Buddhist mandala an image of the Buddha is often represented holding the wheel of the dharma lightly in his hands, "spinning it like a child's toy" in the words of one commentator. The dharma wheel points to that inner principle in us that links our individuality to all of creation — a living principle of order and harmony that holds everything together in unity.

The top that links us to the Creator and creation also links us to one another. If we lose contact with our deep center, represented by the spinning top, our hearts lose affection. We break connection with other human beings. We lose a sense of orientation and direction in our lives.

The links with spiritual guidance are clear. Spiritual guidance is focused on helping people establish an experiential connection to that spinning top, that dynamic spiritual center that links them to God, other human beings, and all creation. Other images could, of course, be used to represent that inner principle. The purpose of spiritual guidance is not to impose a particular image, but to help those who seek guidance to make personal contact with the energy of Spirit in their lives.

The mystics have taught me that spiritual guidance is about seeing, feeling, and listening for that "spinning top" in people. The mystics remind me to notice where joy, life, love, and deep spiritual longing are trying to break through. As a spiritual guide I want to keep my focus on that yearning, that "jack-in-the-box" of spiritual energy that is pressing to be released. As a guide I want to support that yearning, to help those who come for guidance to make a solid connection to it.

I would like to address another thing the mystics can teach us about spiritual guidance and that is the importance of a particular kind of joy. St. Ignatius Loyola describes this joy as "consolation without a cause."[12] Meister Eckhart refers to the same experience as "wandering joy" or "joy without a cause."[13] What Ignatius and Meister Eckhart are referring to is a joy that is experienced at the very foundation of our personal being and perhaps at the foundation of the universe itself. It is the joy of simply being alive, the joy of existence. It is deeper than happiness at getting what I want, finding physical pleasure, or emotional satisfaction in some particular experience. The mystics tell us that if we know joy or consolation without a cause even for a moment, it becomes a touchstone of discernment for the rest of our lives. In that moment we know in our own experience the meaning and purpose of our lives. The breakthrough of the poem about God's spinning top was just such a moment for me. It not only gave a sense of orientation to my personal spiritual journey but also gave me a sense of direction in my work as a spiritual guide.

In spiritual guidance I keep my ears attuned for that special kind of joy, that "consolation without a cause." It may be obscured by fear, anxiety, anger, grief, all kinds of wants, desires and distractions. Underneath all that, I am trying to perceive and connect with the joy at the foundation of a person's being. As spiritual guides I believe we are all invited to take the journey to that inner center where our own freedom and joy are released. Having found that spinning top in our own hearts, we can help others find it as well.

References

Green, Arthur. Rabbi Nahman of Bratslav quoted in *Tormented Master: The Life and Spiritual Quest of Rabbi Nahman of Bratslav.* Tuscaloosa: University of Alabama Press, 1979.

Puhl, S.J., Louis J. (tr.), *The Spiritual Exercises of St. Ignatius.* Westminster, MD: Newman Press, 1963.

Schurmann, Reiner. *Meister Eckhart.* Bloomington, IN: Indiana University Press, 1978.

ALTERNATIVE SETTINGS FOR SPIRITUAL DIRECTION

This fourth section looks at a growing trend to apply spiritual guidance in new areas and with new populations. Mary Ann Scofield, one of the founders of modern spiritual direction, writes of spiritual direction with the poorest of the poor in the slums of Nairobi, with the drug addicts and the homeless in Chicago, Berlin, and other cities. She reminds us of the potentials of the work of spiritual direction for the whole world.

Jürgen Schwing discusses the nature of spiritual guidance and its application to helping the dying in their quest for meaning. Jürgen relates this process to the spiritual teachings of Sri Aurobindo and his three paths of yoga. Bhakti yoga is the path of love and devotion. It applies to working with the dying in celebrating the love in their lives, encouraging forgiveness, and encouraging deeper devotion to God. Jnana yoga is the path of knowledge. This path aids in encouraging the dying to let go of the ego and identify with the deathless Self. Karma yoga is the path of action and service. The dying are often pressed to finish unfinished business, heal relationships, and put their affairs in order. They also need to learn the yogic principle of non-attachment to the outcomes of their actions, as they lose control over their bodies and their lives.

Arthur Hastings discusses his development of the psychomanteum process, an effective and powerful technique for working with grief and bereavement. In this process, individuals spend an hour in front of a mirror in a darkened room. They sit with their feelings and memories of their loved one. Most find their grief becomes eased as they experience a deepening sense of communion with the departed.

Spiritual Guidance on the Margins of Society

We often refer to the Holy One as the center of our lives and the center of all creation. The words come easily but can just as easily be misunderstood. Our faith calls us not to domesticate God into our comfort zone, our "center," but rather to continually uproot ourselves, to willingly leave behind what is familiar, in order to find the God whose "center" is, surprisingly, always on the edges of the world that we know.

Though it may stretch us, it should not surprise us to realize that the Divine is forever moving us more and more toward the poor and marginalized, beyond the pale of proper society. We have seen this in our lifetime with the resurgence of dedication to faith-based social justice work, in liberation theology, in the lives of saints like Dorothy Day and Thomas Merton and Charles de Foucauld. Now we see it emerging in the consciousness of spiritual directors who are bringing their contemplative listening to the edges and forgotten corners of our society.

In the Scriptures we find strong inspiration for this work. The author of the Wisdom of Solomon, for example, writes about Sophia, "Although she is but one, she can do all things, and while remaining in herself, she renews all things; in every generation she passes into holy souls and makes of them friends of God, and prophets; . . ."[14] We've all had the experience of this wisdom passing into and flowing through us. We have probably been very capable spiritual guides when helping our directees to become friends of the Divine, but perhaps not so very good at helping them in a more difficult kind of conversion experience—the kind of spiritual experience that ultimately will put them at odds with a world hostile to the prophets. If our directees stay faithful to the God revealed in Scripture, they will (in God's own time) come to unsettling and inconvenient truths: that our lives of first-world privilege are not tenable unless we share all that we have with the poor, that the corporate and economic and political and religious structures that oppress significant populations must change, that violence and war are never God's way, that reverence for the earth cannot be optional. As spiritual guides, are we prepared to accompany others in this holy transition from friends of God to prophets? Are we ourselves tending the holy in those parts of our milieu where most people seldom think to look for God?

We of course recognize that God's spirit can never be captured or controlled or even predicted. It is never tame or static; it exceeds our expectations. That is the meaning of the above reference from the Book of Wisdom: the spirit passes into holy souls. It is flowing, active. That flow is moving us more and more to be with those on the edges and the margins of our cultures and societies, including our church societies. There is such a longing, among those who are hungering and thirsting, to have someone who will listen contemplatively to their human experience and tend those moments when the mystery of the Divine touches them or breaks into them.

One of my favorite authors is the German theologian Dorothee Soelle. Her book, *The Silent Cry: Mysticism and Resistance,* teaches about spiritual resistance — not in the sense of a directee who might be stonewalling or evading God, but rather in the sense of active communal resistance to unjust social structures. Such communal resistance to injustice is the inevitable consequence of mysticism, and its true touchstone. Dorothee Soelle writes, "There's no experience of the divine that can become so privatized that it remains the property of the owner, the privilege of a person of leisure, the esoteric domain of the initiated."

Authentic experience of the Holy moves us outward; it cannot be hugged as a secret grace. But we Americans seem to prefer the divine in the privacy of our own hearts. Me-and-God spirituality, or in our better moments, God-and-me, is quite strong in our Western world. Contrary to that impulse, the spirit of God is moving us out to the margins to be with people on the edges.

Here are a few examples where spiritual direction is being done on these margins.

1. In the slums of Nairobi, Kenya, there is a woman who is a street-sweeper by day. She works for the city council, and she cleans the streets of downtown Nairobi. At night, though, she offers direction to people who are living in the slums in Methare Valley, one of the worst slums of the city. She and a few other women sit with prostitutes, AIDS widows, and mothers struggling to feed their children. They listen and pray and speak together about God, who is with them in their suffering.

2. In a run-down sector of Berlin, there are spiritual directors sending their retreatants to walk the alleyways where drug addicts, homeless people, and undocumented foreigners live, to be present there to the God who is with the forgotten.

3. A colleague in the United States tells about his spiritual direction interns visiting homes for mentally challenged adults, homeless shelters, and high schools. A priest in Chicago gives retreats to homeless men. This is his full-time ministry.

4. A minister and a spiritual director in Davis, California, spends 20 hours each sitting on a park bench with homeless men and women. She sits with them where they hang out and she listens to their lives.

5. In a dilapidated hotel in the Tenderloin district of San Francisco, there is a room set aside called The Listening Post. Spiritual directors go there to sit and listen to the experience of those suffering from AIDS and HIV. No doubt these homeless people come to the room because there's fresh coffee. But then, over coffee, they begin to talk about their lives and their losses and their longings.

There are many such alternative settings in which spiritual guidance is currently being done. In the first chapter of a book called

Iluminata, Marianne Williamson writes, "There is a spiritual renaissance sweeping the earth. Most people know it, many embrace it, some deny it, and no one can stop it." God's mystery is breaking out in new and unexpected ways, people are getting a little brush or sense of the Divine, and we as spiritual directors need to be there, to tend the Holy. That is our call. That is our blessing.

✿ References

Soelle, Dorothee. *The Silent Cry*: *Mysticism and Resistance.* Minneapolis: Augsburg Fortress, 2001.
Williamson, Marianne. *Iluminata: A Return to Prayer.* New York: Riverhead/Berkley Pub Group, 1994.

Spiritual Guidance at the End of Life

Why me?
Good-bye, my love.
I'm so sorry for hurting you.
I'm afraid I wasted my life.
If only I had more time.
How can I connect with you more deeply?
Please tell me the truth.
I hate being so dependent.
What happens after I die?
Can meditation help me?
Pray for me.
Where is God?
Help me!

Most dying people are grappling with profound questions of meaning. While we all ask such questions, there is something about approaching death that makes them much more compelling and urgent. For the dying person, the quest for meaning and spirituality often takes center stage. In the following pages I share some reflections on providing spiritual guidance with the dying and their families or loved ones. I draw from my own experience working with the dying in their search for meaning and, in the second half of this paper, from Sri Aurobindo's philosophy and spiritual practice. I tell several stories of individuals I have worked with. While I have changed names and some circumstances to protect their identities, the stories are not composites but true stories.

The Search for Meaning and the Mystery Beyond

I'll start by defining some important terms. There are as many definitions of spirituality as there are spiritual seekers. In my work with the
dying, I have provided spiritual guidance to people from a very wide
variety of religious and spiritual orientations, including those that
define themselves as humanists, agnostics, or atheists. For the purpose
of this article, therefore, I define spirituality in two ways. First, and
more generally, spirituality can be defined for humanists (including
agnostics and atheists) as the existential search for meaning. While
humanists do not accept the existence of a God or Higher Being, they
seek spiritual support because they understand that death is more
than a physical event and that their state of mind makes a difference
in the amount of suffering or peace they experience. Second, for
many others, spirituality is about what lies beyond body and mind —
some type of Spirit, Higher Self, Transcendent Source, or Mystery.
Spirituality in this second sense can be defined as the search for Spirit
or the Mystery Beyond.

Spiritual Guidance

I use the words "spiritual direction," "spiritual guidance," and "spiritual companionship" interchangeably. In the broadest sense, spiritual
direction, guidance, or companionship for humanists can be called
"deep listening" or "existential listening" and involves being present to
and helping clarify the inner movements of a person's thoughts and
feelings in her quest for meaning.

The traditional definition of spiritual direction relates to working
with someone with the explicit understanding that the work is done
in relation to God, the Divine, or Higher Self. Spiritual direction is
defined as "holy listening" or "one person's (the director) being prayerfully present to another (the directee) as together they seek to discern
the action of the Holy Spirit in the latter's life"[15] I basically work within
this classical approach, but expand it in three ways. First, in providing

holy listening, I listen not only prayerfully but also contemplatively and soulfully. Second, I listen to the presence of Spirit in the directee's life not only as Holy Spirit (a Christian term) but also in its many other manifestations, for example, as the Beloved, the Holy Mother, Shiva/Shakti, the Holy One, Emptiness, or whatever manifestation presents itself or most deeply resonates with the directee. And finally, I offer spiritual direction not only one-on-one but also in groups, either formally or informally, often at a dying patient's home.

The terms "spiritual director" and "spiritual guide" are somewhat of a misnomer. In the practice of holy listening, I am not the director or guide, but Spirit is. I am the holy listener, trying to help the directee to hear and understand Spirit's presence in her life. However, before we delve into a deeper discussion of traditional spiritual direction, let's start by exploring spiritual companionship for humanists (which include atheists and agnostics).

Spiritual Companionship for the Humanist

Spiritual direction always starts with presence. The best way to engage a dying person in facing the profound questions of meaning she is struggling with is by simply being fully present with her in an authentic and compassionate way.

When I teach aspiring spiritual guides, I always find general agreement and head nodding when I introduce this concept and practice. Most of the time, however, it also turns out to be the most difficult for new companions to the dying.

Many of us who appear perfectly relaxed, compassionate, and articulate in most situations can get insecure and nervous when sitting with the dying. There are several reasons. First, we tend to carry the results of our culture's fear and avoidance of death in our bones. We don't have much contact with death or with dying people. We don't know what to say, what to ask, or where to begin. Second, new guides tend to get hung up on the supposed sacredness or spiritual nature of their role. They feel they have to fix things or make them better and as a result simply try too hard. And finally, sitting with the dying is different from your regular hour-long conversation with an articulate directee. The dying person may be in pain. Health care professionals or family members may interrupt you. The directee may talk very slowly and in a less than coherent way because of medications she is taking or brain metastases that effect her thinking and speaking.

It is then especially important to stress the "companionship" aspect of our work. The word "companion" comes from the Latin *cum* (with) and *panis* (bread). A companion is someone we break bread with. Our first task is simply to be a friend, to be there, to sit with, and to accompany.

The following are helpful guidelines for helping the dying in their quest for meaning:

- When talking to a dying person, be fully present, authentic, and genuinely compassionate.

- Listen deeply and with curiosity. Truly hear the person's deepest needs.

- Do not think your way into a spiritual connection, but trust your intuition and let your heart open.

- Understand the dying person's need for love. Embody love; don't just talk about it. Acknowledge, celebrate, and encourage love between the person and his or her family or friends.

- Understand the dying person's need for self-worth. Affirm and truly express your appreciation for all that is beautiful and courageous in him or her.

- Allow the person to grieve. He or she is losing so much. Allow tears to flow if they want to. They move grief through and make room inside.

- Don't lose your sense of humor. Laughter is good medicine, even and especially at the end of life.

- Don't force a solution to psycho-spiritual problems. Allow for the solution to emerge in its own good time.

- Sometimes there are no "solutions." We are not always here to fix things, but to offer our compassion and caring presence.

- Support the person in becoming authentic at the end of life. He or she may "drop the mask" or "stop the games" and express a desire to be truthful, honest, and authentic.

- Cultivate gratitude. Encourage the person to share what he or she is most grateful for. Help the person to say his or her "thank you."

- Cultivate forgiveness. None of us is perfect, but forgiveness can heal many wounds.

- Help the person and family to say their "good-byes." Help them express how much they'll miss each other. Help them to let each other know they'll be okay. Allow the family to say to the person, "It's okay. You can let go. I love you."

- Plan a memorial service, celebration of life, funeral, or other ritual with the dying person while he or she is still alive. Allow him or her to feel how comforting this will be for the family and loved ones.

- When the person gets close to dying, protect him or her from too many visitors or intrusions.

- Create a spiritual environment that is inspiring and comforting for the person and his or her loved ones (music, candles, flowers, photos, inspirational readings, and so on).

- Encourage family and loved ones to shift their focus from doing to being. Model and teach the value of simple presence.

- Sit in silence. Embrace not knowing. Breathe.

- Learn to love ever more deeply.

- Learn from your mistakes. Allow yourself to grow.

- Be gentle with yourself. Take good care of yourself.

- Know that it is a privilege to be let into someone's dying.

- Let the dying teach you how to live.

- Share with the living what you learn from the dying.

- Prepare for your own dying.

Finding Personal Meaning

As we accompany the dying humanist through his final months, weeks, and days, we help his process of finding meaning – not the meaning of life in the abstract, but his personal meaning. We help him find answers for questions like these: "Was I true to myself?" "Did I love well?" "Will anyone remember me?" "Did I accomplish anything of lasting value?" We help by being a witness, by celebrating his accomplishments and successes, grieving his losses, and helping carry his regrets. We affirm the love he has shared and witness the special moments that carry deep meaning. The director can ask careful questions leading the directee to reflect on the legacy he wants to leave for those he is surviving. With this perspective, even losses and disappointments become lessons he can impart to the next generation.

The Search for Spirit, God, or the Mystery

We now move from discussing spiritual direction for humanists to delving into spiritual direction for those who see themselves in relationship to some kind of transcendent Being, Spirit, or Mystery Beyond. The guidelines discussed above apply here also, but there are additional considerations I would like to explore.

In my own search for Spirit, God, or the Mystery, I have expanded my traditional Christian roots by studying Eastern and Western mystical paths. My introduction to yoga came through practice with and initiation by a teacher of kundalini and *sahaja* (spontaneously arising) yoga. Because an important part of this path involves physical exercises, it is hard to apply to work with the dying. I have come to value the philosophy and spiritual practice of Sri Aurobindo's integral yoga in my work as a spiritual guide. In the following discussion I show how his integral yoga can be deeply helpful when adapted for work with the dying in the West.

The Four Aids and the Triple Path of Integral Spirituality

I am not offering here a systematic exposition or analysis of Aurobindo's system, which is compiled in thirty volumes of collected works. Rather, I only adapt several of his main principles to my purpose of spiritual guidance for the dying. I receive inspiration from what he calls the "Four Aids" and the "Triple Path," as described in *The Synthesis of Yoga* and *The Integral Yoga*.

The Four Aids, according to Aurobindo, are a summary of the essential guidelines needed to grow into the truth and power of Spirit. The first aid is the *shastra*, "the knowledge of the truths, principles, powers and processes" of the integral yoga.[16] In the following paragraph, he summarizes his *shastra*, talking about himself in the third person:

> The teaching of Sri Aurobindo starts from that of the ancient sages of India: that behind the appearances of the universe there is the reality of a being and consciousness, a self of all things, one and eternal. All beings are united in that one self and spirit but divided by a certain separativity of consciousness, an ignorance of their true self and reality in the mind, life, and body. It is possible by a certain psychological discipline to remove this veil of separative consciousness and become aware of the true Self, the divinity within us and all.[17] The psychological discipline that removes the veil and lets us become aware of our true Self, which

is the divinity within us (at the core of our own soul) and within all (at the center of all that exists in this world), is his integral yoga. The integral yoga is his unique integration of the traditional yogas of knowledge (*jnana*), devotion (*bhakti*), and action (*karma*), known as the Triple Path.

Becoming aware of and identifying with this Self requires the difficult process of disidentifying from ego. The spiritual practices of the Triple Path are designed to move beyond ego to Self. "[The ego's] surrender to that which transcends it is its liberation from bonds and limits and its perfect freedom."[18]

The second aid is personal effort or spiritual practice. The central principle of this effort or practice is one's surrender to the Divine directly, a complete "consecration" of one's whole being: "The Sadhaka (student, aspirant) must become conscious that a force other than his own, a force transcending his egoistic endeavor and capacity, is at work in him and to this Power he learns progressively to submit himself and delivers up to it the charge of his Yoga."[19] He also says: "Surrender means to consecrate everything in oneself to the Divine . . ., to live for the Divine and not for the ego."[20]

The third aid is the inner guide or teacher: "The full recognition of this inner Guide, Master of the Yoga, lord, light, enjoyer and goal of all . . . effort, is of the utmost importance." This inner guide appears to different people in different ways. It may appear as "an impersonal Wisdom, Love and Power behind all things, as an Absolute manifesting in the relative and attracting it, as one's highest Self and the highest Self of all, as a Divine Person within us and in the world, in one of his – or her – numerous forms and names or as the ideal which the mind conceives."[21]

Most people, Aurobindo suggests, need an external teacher, such as a prophet, an avatar, or a guru. He suggests making use of whatever image of the Divine or whatever human manifestation of the Divine is available to one or attracts one, but makes clear that one should not devote oneself to external aids, but only to the Divine directly. The integral student should not "forget the aim of these external aids which is to awaken his soul to the Divine within him."[22]

The fourth and final aid is time. While the ego tends to see time, or the lack thereof, as an obstacle, the Divine uses time as an instrument. It is the medium and condition within which we journey toward Spirit and then allow Spirit to transform us. The relation to time becomes especially poignant at the end of life. While the ego sees time as running out, the deeper Self sees the slowing down of the activities of the body and mind as contributing to a deeper opening to the presence of Spirit.

Aurobindo's integral yoga combines the yogas of love and devotion (*bhakti*), of service and action (*karma*), and of self-knowledge (*jnana*) in what he calls the Triple Path. This Triple Path is called "integral" for several reasons. First, it integrates the traditionally separate yogas of devotion, service, and self-knowledge. Second, it integrates a non-dual understanding of the Divine with a dual one. In other words, the integral yogi sees and experiences the Divine as both formless Spirit and as a Divine Person. Furthermore, the integral yogi seeks to integrate the various manifestations of the Personal Divine – not only Krishna, but also Christ; not only Kali, but also Kwan Yin, etcetera. Most important, the integral yogi does not escape into union with the Divine by renouncing the world (like in the traditional yogas), but integrates nature and the Divine. Indeed, she aims at entering into the Divine and then bringing it down into this life, transforming the outer being of the personality through the power of the divinity within, und ultimately transforming and divinizing this world. The integral yogi seeks to be a channel for the Divine Self-expression: "To grow into the truth and power of the Spirit and by the direct action of that power to be made a fit channel of its self-expression, — a living of [humanity] in the Divine and a divine living of the Spirit in humanity, — will therefore be the principle and the whole object of an integral Yoga."[23]

The Path of Love and Devotion

> The nature of Bhakti is adoration, worship, self-offering to what
> is greater than oneself; the nature of love is a feeling or a seeking
> for closeness and union.
>   Bhakti . . . is a state of the heart and soul.[24]

Each of the three yogas in Aurobindo's Triple Path takes a human
capacity or power and develops it beyond its usual limits. In the path
of bhakti yoga, we start by tending and deepening the power of love
and devotion to our loved ones. In traditional bhakti yoga, the yogi
sublimates his love for other human beings and the world into love
for God alone. She is then lost to the world in her merging into the
Divine. In Aurobindo's integral understanding of bhakti, however,
love for the Divine does not replace love for humans. Instead, opening ourselves more deeply to the Divine in any of its forms opens us
to the reality that all of life is an expression of the Divine. In and
through all beings, we love the Divine.

"Such love . . . loves God and is one with him in all his being, and
therefore in all beings, and to work for the world is then to feel and
fulfill . . . one's love for God."[25]

For Aurobindo, bhakti yoga proceeds by devotion to "the One who
is differently named and imaged by the religions."[26] The spiritual
guide is encouraged in her own practice to devote herself to the many
manifestations of the Divine, for example, as Allah, Yahweh, or
Goddess, or as Christ, Krishna, Kali, or Kwan Yin. In doing so, the
spiritual director is then able to help many different directees in their
devotional journeys, whatever they may be.

The integral yogi studies the scriptures of many traditions but
knows that each of them is only a partial expression of the Divine: "In
the end he . . . must live in his own soul beyond the written Truth. . . .
For he is not the Sadhaka of a book or many books; he is the Sadhaka
of the Infinite."[27] In other words, he is a devotee not of a tradition, but
of the Divine directly.

Furthermore, the guide is encouraged to let the Divine be revealed in her and through her. In the words of Aurobindo, "It is not sufficient to worship Krishna, Christ or Buddha without, if there is not the revealing and the formation of the Buddha, the Christ or Krishna in ourselves." [28] Ideally, the spiritual guide can become for the directee, however imperfect, an incarnation of the Divine.

In spiritual guidance for the dying, we can apply these bhakti practices in various ways:

- Celebrate the love that is already there in the directee and her relationships.

- Encourage practices such as forgiveness, gratitude, and reconciliation that create more love and loving relationships.

- Introduce and encourage practices that help the directee develop a deeper devotion to God, Spirit, or Higher Power.

- Encourage the patient to deepen within her own tradition, if she has one, and/or to explore other paths and forms of the Divine if she feels so inclined.

- Explore the Divine Feminine as well as the Divine Masculine.

- Offer prayer and end-of-life ritual.

- Sing or chant, together or individually.

- Read sacred scriptures that are meaningful to the directee.

- Facilitate centering prayer or other forms of contemplative practices.

- Teach forms of meditation that open the heart and promote compassion, such as *metta* meditation or *tonglen*.

Dorothy's Story: Tenderly

Dorothy was in her mid-eighties and had been diagnosed with terminal cancer when I first met her in her home, together with her husband, Henry, and one of their adult daughters. She was very direct: "I know I'm dying. I have no idea how I'm going to do that. It's important for me to die with dignity. I'm not a religious person, but I feel that I'm going to need a sense of spirituality to pull that off. Can you help me with that?"

I responded: "I'll do my very best. I'm not going to have some easy answers, though. I'll be more of a companion, trying to help you find your own spirituality."

I visited Dorothy weekly at her home. She told me about her life, her family, her illness, and hospice care. I listened deeply, trying to understand her deepest needs and wishes. I also listened for the presence of spirit. Dorothy said that she had been raised in the Episcopal Church. She had liked the ritual but felt that the doctrines didn't speak to her. When she became an adult, she left the church because it didn't seem relevant anymore. She hadn't been to a church in decades.

Approaching Dorothy's home, I first noticed a large, round rock at her front door. It had an inscription: "Dorothy and Henry, 50 Years of Love and Happiness."

Dorothy lit up when talking about her husband and children. Sensing that her heart and the path of devotion were going to be the opening to her spirituality, I was looking for a way to let her heart speak. "Dorothy," I said, "you know that I am about to get married, and I'm curious. You've been married for so long, and you and Henry are so obviously happy with each other. What's the secret of your love, and how have you made it work for fifty years?" Dorothy got a big smile on her face and gladly shared: "First of all, never take love for granted, especially not after fifty years. I'm telling Henry every day I love him, and I find special ways to let him know."

"Second, the small things are important in love," she explained. One day we were sitting in her living room, she in an armchair and I on the sofa. "My back is rather sore, would you mind handing me a pillow?" she asked. I handed her a pillow from the sofa, which she put behind her back. We continued our conversation, but after a while she couldn't resist telling me: "The small things are important. It would have been so nice if you hadn't just handed me the pillow but had placed it behind my back, making sure I was comfortable. Always remember that with your wife!

"Third, never neglect the physical aspect of love," she taught me. "I'm a real snuggler, and Henry appreciates that." Dorothy also reminded me that it was important to express your love in creative ways. She shared poems she had written for special occasions, like her daughters' twenty-first birthdays or her husband's fiftieth birthday. And finally, she shared her and Henry's love song, "Tenderly," as well as the history behind that song. When they were newlyweds, they had stayed at a bed-and-breakfast, trying to go to sleep early. Below their room was the bar, and the jukebox kept playing "Tenderly" over and over again. What had been an annoyance at first eventually turned into their love song and was played during many special occasions.

As her teaching about love unfolded over the weeks, I reflected back to her: "Dorothy, the way you have embraced love and have made love real in your everyday life is quite extraordinary. To me, your ability to love, to kindle romance, to celebrate intimate connection is a deep spirituality, if only you could claim it as that."

With my encouragement, Dorothy came to embrace her ability for love, for romance, and for creative expression as her spirituality. Over time, she came to value her life and her gift for love and intimate connection as grounded in something larger than herself. She came to embrace her loving as an expression and manifestation of a more universal force, something that she began to call "God" again and that she was experiencing as deeply spiritual and sacred now. She began to open to the Divine.

While Dorothy became physically weaker over the period of weeks and months that I visited, she felt a deepening sense of spirituality. She continued to surrender herself into the presence and guidance of Spirit. When I made my last visit to Dorothy, she was in a semi-comatose state, unable to talk but able to hear and understand. Henry and their daughters were worried. Her limbs were shaking in tremors, and her eyelashes were fluttering. To her family, she seemed very distressed.

I sat in silence for some time with Dorothy and Henry. I listened to Henry's sadness and affirmed the bond of love they shared and the grief he was feeling. Henry asked me to say a prayer. Opening myself to the power of divine love, of which Dorothy was such a beautiful and unique manifestation, I said something like this: "Holy One, Spirit of Love, I give thanks for Dorothy and her life. I give thanks for her joyful and compassionate spirit and her generous heart that has touched so many. I give thanks for the many blessings she's enjoyed: the love of her husband Henry for over fifty years, their two beautiful daughters to whom they gave life, and their grandchildren.

"I give thanks for their love song, 'Tenderly,' and that she was able to experience and share so much love and tenderness in her life. Please let her transition tenderly from this life to the life to come. Surround and infuse her with your love and light. Forgive her any of her shortcomings, for none of us is perfect, but your love and forgiveness are always greater. Let her know deep inside that she has lived well and loved well. May Dorothy know that Henry and her whole family will be okay and that they are ready to let her go when she feels ready. Tenderly, please, take her tenderly. Amen."

I kissed Dorothy gently on her forehead and said good-bye. After that visit, according to the family, she was physically completely at peace and stayed that way until she died two or three days later.

The Path of Knowledge

The path of knowledge, *jnana* yoga, is best suited for seekers with a reflective or intellectual bent. Traditionally, *jnana* yoga engages the seeker in spiritual study and reflection and eventually in the realization that the only true reality is the Divine Self and that our phenomenal existence is only maya, a delusion of our mind. Intellectual understanding is not enough but is the beginning step toward a deeper realization of one's whole being. Through meditative practice the seeker shifts identification from his ego to his own deeper Self, which is at the same time the Divine Self at the core of and beyond all phenomenal existence. In traditional jnana yoga, once this realization is achieved, the seeker abides in the eternal peace of the Divine Self, oblivious to and no longer related to this world of maya.

The integral yogi, however, in realizing the eternal Self as the Source of this world, which is intimately related to it, shifts identification from his limited ego toward the Self without denying the world but now able to see it as the manifestation of the Divine.

Dying involves letting go of the ego and merging into the Self, and jnana practices can facilitate this process. A skilled guide may help a directee by applying the jnana technique of discernment. In this discernment, the directee learns that his anxious thoughts or overwhelming feelings are not an expression of his true Self. In meditation he may learn to quiet his thoughts and feelings and get in touch with the deeper peace of his true Self. At other times, someone caught in the headiness and detachment of jnana yoga may need to be reminded to ground his spiritual practice in his life.

Transforming Escapist Spirituality

Tim was an extremely devoted jnana yogi. Hundreds of mystical books filled bookshelves in his bedroom, kitchen, and living room in a small and dilapidated apartment. Dusty statues and pictures of holy beings were everywhere. He loved discussing spiritual philosophy every chance he got. He had studied with renowned spiritual teachers in the U.S. and during trips to India. He meditated six hours every day.

Tim was also addicted to an escapist spirituality and in need of learning about integrating the Divine with this world and letting it empower his life and relationships. "Look at this apple," he said in one of our conversations, "if you leave it sitting here, it will rot. That's the nature of this world. It's all rotten. I strive to attain union with the Divine, which alone is real."

Then one day Tim's life partner, Dana, with whom he had lived in their apartment for the last fifteen years, was diagnosed with a fast growing cancer. They were told there were no more treatments that offered any hope for survival. It was devastating for both of them. Dana entered our hospice program.

These events turned their lives upside down. Dana had been doing most of the housework, allowing Tim the time and energy to devote to his spiritual practice. Now she needed his help, and Tim was overwhelmed with the tasks of being the primary caregiver. He needed to wash her, feed her, give her medications, and change her diapers.

The hospice team was very upset with Tim, who simply did not do well providing for Dana's needs. Often, he would not give her the meds in time. Once, the nurse discovered that Dana had been lying in her own urine and feces for hours while Tim was meditating in the room next door.

In turn, Tim was mad at the nurses and other hospice workers. He felt they were judgmental toward him and Dana, not accepting their preference for more alternative treatments and philosophies, and pushing traditional drugs and attitudes on them. In my conversations with him, he opened up about how overwhelmed and depressed he felt.

I thought it would be helpful to build a relationship of trust with him by engaging him in what he loved. This was not hard, because I was intrigued by his spiritual life, and we shared a deep interest in the mystical paths of many traditions. At the same time, I was mindful of the deeper need, namely, for him to devote himself to the care of Dana and to transform his spirituality from an escapist to a more integral one. "I know I'm not doing a good job taking care of Dana," he said, "but I don't want to hurt her. I am trying my best. It's just that if I don't have the time to do my spiritual practice, I get off center and I'm not doing well."

After offering a good dose of empathy, I suggested: "Tim, maybe it's time to broaden your spiritual practice. You are doing really well turning your mind toward the Divine, but I think you need to learn to open your heart also. You look at taking care of Dana as a distraction from your spiritual practice, when really it is an opportunity to open to Spirit even more fully. I think you are invited to open yourself to the path of devotion by serving the Divine in her incarnation of your beloved, your Dana."

He thought about it for a while and then responded: "I haven't thought about it this way, but maybe you are right."

We had several conversations along this line, but things got worse before they got better. Tim threatened and yelled at one of the nurses, and he and Dana were discharged from hospice because of it. Eventually, they came back to hospice, and after this break, the nurses reported a deep shift in Tim. He became a much more capable caregiver, treated the nurses with more respect, and showed a more vulnerable side. Serving Dana the best that he could now became the focus of his life and spirituality. I saw him speak tenderly to her, cry for her, and deeply care for her well-being. Dana was a deeply spiritual being in her own right, more devotionally oriented. I had asked her what form of the Divine most deeply spoke to her. She said that Kwan Yin, the Goddess of Compassion, as well as the loving gaze of the Buddha, most filled her with a sense of the loving presence of Spirit. One of the most touching end-of-life rituals I ever engaged in was sharing an essential *phowa* meditation for Dana.[29] When Dana was close to dying, Tim and I prayed together and then visualized the presence of Kwan Yin in front of and above her. We visualized a radiant light streaming from her presence, surrounding and filling Dana, and then lifting her up and merging her into her own loving presence. A few days later, Dana died in peace, well taken care of by her beloved.

The Path of Action and Service

Karma yoga, the path of action and service, proceeds by transforming the power of will that the seeker uses to act in the world. The karma yogi seeks to withdraw his will from identification with his ego and to align it with his higher Self. There are two ways to travel the path of karma yoga, depending on one's predisposition toward either a reflective or an emotional attitude. The more emotionally oriented person is likely to practice karma yoga devotionally, surrendering his life's activity to a personal Divine. "Not my will, but Thine be done" is his motto. He seeks guidance from Spirit and performs his actions in surrender to and powered by this higher will. He becomes an instrument or channel of Spirit.

The more intellectually predisposed seeker practices in the spirit of non-attachment. Trying to avoid ego involvement with his work, which only distracts him from identification with the Self, he practices non-attachment to the fruits of his works.

The dying often feel pressure to complete unfinished business, to heal relationships, and to get their affairs in order. They face difficult choices under a lot of pressure and often feel lost. The skilled guide can help them open to Divine guidance and surrender themselves, and their living and dying, into God's hands (or the Divine presence, understood in their own way).

The practice of non-attachment to the outcome of one's action also can be especially helpful at the end of life. The dying person loses so much control, even over his own body. Learning that consciously surrendering control over one's life (and death) is not only an option, but indeed a spiritual practice, may provide a better perspective.

I have often seen the dying go through a re-evaluation of their priorities. Instead of searching for success or recognition, they now cherish the opportunity to do as much good as they still can. They shower those around them with love and attention, out of their own realization of the preciousness of their relationships. They find healing in selfless service to those around them.

Service in the Shamanic Mode

Susan opened into a deeper experience of Spirit through a heartbreaking ordeal. After a marriage that had ended in divorce, and now in her fifties, Susan's search for her soul mate had finally been answered. She was elated after finding the love of her life and getting married in a beautiful ceremony at the ocean.

Only weeks into their marriage, her husband suffered a debilitating stroke. The resulting paralysis of his body was very severe and threw him into depression and hopelessness. Unable to bear his despair, he started drinking again, succumbing to an old addiction that he had worked hard to overcome. Susan tried as best she could to console and support her beloved. Eventually she realized, though, that he was drinking himself to death. Still deeply connected to him, she considered his dying wish: "Die with me."

Reflecting back on this time, she said she gave it some serious thought, but eventually told him: "I cannot die with you. There is more for me in this life that I have to do." After his death, she cycled through deep grief, and when coming through the worst of it and starting to feel a little better, she told herself: "Now I better get real about what it is that I said I needed to do." Susan, a research assistant, had long had a yearning for a deeper spiritual life, and now was the time to get real. She also felt a deep desire for service, for making a real difference in people's lives. Since then, she has devoted herself to an intensive multiyear training and apprenticeship with an indigenous Latin American shaman. For Susan, this shamanic apprenticeship has required many sacrifices. It has deepened her commitment to a path of service and surrender to guidance from the spirit world. It has given her many gifts, which she is now sharing in her work as a spiritual companion with the dying in our program. While keeping her daytime job, she teaches and leads workshops about the use of ritual and ceremony for healing.

Conclusion

The dying are in need of companions who can skillfully provide spiritual guidance for them on their final journeys. In the first part of this discussion I have suggested guidelines for helping the dying in their quest for meaning. These guidelines are applicable for anyone at the end of life asking basic existential questions, not only for those searching for a connection with a Spirit or some kind of Higher

Power. In the second part I have applied Sri Aurobindo's Triple Path for work with the dying in the West. Dying involves a process of letting go of one's ego and ego-based involvement in this life and merging into Spirit or Self. I suggest that the processes and practices of bhakti/devotion, jnana/self-knowledge, and karma/selfless action can facilitate this process of letting go. Working with the dying is both challenging and rewarding. When we are willing and able to accompany them in their final transformation, the dying teach us profound lessons about love, surrender, and opening to the Mystery.

 References

Aurobindo, Sri. *The Synthesis of Yoga*. Twin Lakes, WI: Lotus Light Publications, 1996.

Aurobindo, Sri. *Integral Yoga: Sri Aurobindo's Teaching and Method of Practice*. Pondicherry, India: Sri Aurobindo Ashram Trust, 1993.

Aurobindo, Sri. *The Essential Aurobindo,* edited by Robert McDermott. Great Barrington, MA: Lindisfarne Press, 1987.

Doka, Kenneth J. with John D. Morgan, Editors. *Death and Spirituality.* Amityville, NY: Baywood Publishing Company, 1993.

Guenther, Margaret. "Companions at the Threshold: Spiritual Direction with the Dying," in: *Presence*, Volume 6, No. 3, September 2000, pp. 29-39.

Kübler-Ross, Elisabeth. *On Death and Dying*. New York, NY: Simon & Schuster, 1969.

Longaker, Christine. *Facing Death and Finding Hope: A Guide to the Emotional and Spiritual Care of the Dying*. New York: Broadway Books, 1997.

Merton, Thomas. "Thomas Merton on Spiritual Direction," edited by Elizabeth G. Stout with assistance from Dr. Paul M. Pearson, in: *Presence*, Vol. 9, No. 3, October 2003, pp. 39-43.

Pandit, M.P. *Sadhana in Sri Aurobindo's Yoga*. Sri Aurobindo Ashram, Pondicherry, India: Dipti Publications, 1971.

Rinpoche, Sogyal. *The Tibetan Book of Living and Dying*. San Francisco: HarperCollins, 1992.

Segal, Suzanne. *Collision with the Infinite: A Life Beyond the Personal Self.* San Diego: New Dove Press, 1996.

Smith, Douglas C. *Caregiving: Hospice-Proven Techniques for Healing Body and Soul.* New York: Macmillan, 1997.

Smith, Houston. *The Illustrated World's Religions: A Guide to Our Wisdom Traditions.* San Francisco: HarperCollins, 1994.

A New Approach to Grief Work

The psychomanteum process for bereavement is a recently developed approach for addressing grief, sadness, unresolved feelings, and other effects from the death of a friend, relative, or loved one. In our research at the Institute of Transpersonal Psychology, we have taken more than one hundred twenty-five bereaved persons through a structured process in which they remember the deceased, sit in a psychomanteum — which is a quiet, darkened booth — and reflect on their feelings about the deceased. More than 90 percent of the people who go through the process report a reduction in their feelings of bereavement. More than half say they have felt the presence of the deceased, and often tell of conversations or communication with the person who has died.[30]

A psychomanteum is a dimly lit, curtained booth, with a mirror at one end to focus attention and a comfortable chair. The bereaved person sits in the chair and looks at the mirror. The mirror is tilted so it reflects darkness rather than the viewer's face. The booth is thus dark and quiet. This creates a mild altered state of consciousness in which the person can bring back memories, and reflect on feelings about the relationship and the death. The psychomanteum was developed by Dr. Raymond Moody, who is familiar as the researcher who coined the term "Near Death Experience."[31]

Moody states that this is a modern version of the ancient Greek oracles of the dead. Research with the psychomanteum has been limited, but shows that the participants often have a sense of presence of the deceased, insights and changes in bereavement feelings, and unusual physical and sensory phenomena.[32] The booth itself can be considered a form of sensory deprivation, now known as Restricted Sensory Environmental Therapy. [33]

Three Stages of the Psychomanteum Process

We use the psychomanteum as one part of a three-stage structured process that takes about three hours. In the first stage of the process, the person sits with a facilitator, who asks them to talk about the person who has died. The facilitator asks questions such as, "What are your feelings about this person? If you could speak to her, what would you say? What are your unfinished feelings about her?" This is a period of remembering the person, reflecting on feelings about the death, and the loss of the relationship. The facilitator is not doing therapy or counseling. There is no probing into dynamics of the loss, or giving of advice on how to deal with the death. Rather, the facilitator helps remember the past and express the present. We are just listening and being open to their experience. This is not a mechanical process. At the end of this interview, we offer art materials and suggest that the participant use colors and drawings to express feelings in that nonverbal mode. Most try this, sometimes saying that they are not artists.

Our participants fill out a questionnaire before the process, which includes a checklist of bereavement effects. The strongest effects participants report are the need to communicate, to improve their relationship with the deceased, sadness, unresolved feelings, grief, loss, and guilt.

In the second stage of the process, the bereaved person sits in the psychomanteum booth. The participant is told just to look into the mirror, think about the person who has died, think about what he or she would like to say, remember memories and feelings, and be open to what happens. Moody developed the psychomanteum as a possible way of getting contact with apparitions of people who had died, and reported that twenty-five percent of his early subjects to eighty-five percent of his later subjects felt the presence of the deceased. In our recruitment information and consent form, we are explicit that they can seek a connection with the deceased. Thus, this is usually in participants' minds when they come, but we ask them simply to be open to any sensation, feeling, or thought that happens, whether or not anything seems to indicate the presence of the person. The participants sit in the psychomanteum for about forty five minutes, with the facilitator in a room next to the psychomanteum room. Then they come back to the room they were in before, and they talk about what happened. That is the third stage and the end of the structured process.

What happens while they are inside this room? What is their experience? They often begin by feeling rather anxious: Am I doing it right? Is something going to happen? After a few minutes some sensory phenomena may occur. Flashes or streams of light may occur. The mirror may cloud over or disappear. Images may appear in the mirror, outside the mirror, or in their subjective mental space. Usually participants are thinking about the person who has died. The memories of the deceased may continue. One participant said "I have never had forty five minutes just to think about my brother. That is amazing in itself."

Half or more of the people that we take through say they have felt the presence of the person who has died. Participants frequently report mental dialog with the deceased person, and feel they are given a message, verbally or in a feeling. Smells have been reported–the pipe tobacco of a grandfather, the cosmetic powder of a grandmother, and the smell of candy associated with a brother. We do not interpret these experiences, but leave it up to the person to decide the meaning of what happens.

The deceased ones being sought include parents, children who have died before their parents, aunts, uncles, grandmothers, grandfathers. It may be a lost twin. It may be a child or parent who has committed suicide. We have had people come through seeking to help bereavement feelings with pets who have died; two cats, a dog, and two horses have been the lost ones, and some of the participants felt a sense of their presence.

After sitting in the booth, the participant returns with the facilitator for an integrative interview, talking about the experience and what its meaning is for the bereaved. After the interview, the participant is invited to use the art materials again. Usually we find that the before and after artwork shows dramatic shifts in color, tone, and content.

Experiences in the Booth

Let me summarize some accounts from people who went through the psychomanteum process. One sixty-five-year old woman said: "This experience really allowed me to reconnect with my grandfather. I feel I was also able to see some of his qualities that I would really like to reconnect with in myself, such as humor and authenticity."

A woman whose daughter had died unexpectedly in high school told us: "I have cried for her every day since she died four years ago." Her daughter, she said, came to her and said, "Mother, I can't come to you when you cry. If you can stop crying and be happy, I can come to you." This was extremely reassuring to the mother.

Another person wanted to contact her spiritual teacher who died unexpectedly in an accident a decade before. He was the spiritual leader of a group, which continued after his death. She said that he came to her, talked with her, and gave her specific instructions as to what she was now to do with the group. He gave her a message to give to his successor, and he told her that she was to work with the children in the group. It was a very long and extensive communication.

A young man wrote, "I entered a very meditative and peaceful state in which my eyes would alternate between gazing in the mirror and soft eyes. Close to the end, I heard a Beethoven piano concerto playing in my head. My dad was a very good pianist and was very capable of playing Beethoven. I had an image or memory of my father playing his piano like he used to do when I was young. I felt very peaceful the entire fifty minutes. I started to think about my dad and some of the moments we shared, mostly images of him smiling. I told him internally that I appreciated his kind spirit, gentleness and good-natured presence. I did this with my hands joined together at the palms as if I were praying. I was wondering what his hands looked like when I felt his hands over mine. It seemed eerie but that went away, and I began playing with what I was experiencing."

In these accounts, we are bound by research ethics. It is important for us to make sure our clients understand that even if we share experiences, their identities remain confidential. There is no publication of people's names or their experiences in any way that would invade their privacy or disclose who they are. In this article, circumstances and identities are changed to protect the participant.

Some participants who go through the process do not have that kind of explicit contact but they tend return from this experience with a shift in the level of their bereavement and feelings of resolution. In our last one hundred subjects, all but eight showed reductions in their bereavement scores on the questionnaires.

Spiritual Guidance

The question now might be: where does spiritual guidance come in? Spiritual guidance does not come in with us giving them advice, interpreting their experience, or saying it was or wasn't their father. Participants are not hesitant to express their doubts and to wonder about what happened. Some of the people who go through say, "I don't know if it was my grandmother or if I was making it up in my mind." We say, "You have to decide for yourself. What did it seem like? What was it like for you?" The uncertainty does not seem to stop people from changing their feelings.

This is not therapy. We are not analyzing them. This is not medication. We do not tell them to take Prozac. It is not a support group. This is an *experience* that changes them. Listening to their feelings openly and acceptingly is healing in itself. One of our faculty members sat in the psychomanteum and said, "I understand what you are doing. You are reversing the defenses." Listening to their memories and feelings relieves the need to repress bereavement feelings. In this Western, industrialized culture, there are taboos against showing strong feelings for deaths. I think that many people raise defenses against those feelings because of the social expectation of getting on with your life, and because these feelings are painful. Loss is painful. The result is that the self does not have the opportunity to feel the feelings and come to terms with them in a natural way.

There are two major theoretical perspectives on bereavement counseling.[34] One, based on object relations theory, holds that people who grieve should be encouraged to release their connections to the deceased, and they should reconfigure their lives without the bonds to the person who has died. Perhaps they feel that is expected and, it is unnatural to grieve excessively. The other perspective is that, though the deceased is no longer alive and with the person, it is all right for the relationship to continue, but in a different way, and the bonds of connection can still have a place in one's life. With our participants we usually see the second pattern, that of a relationship that continues, but in a changed way. But even so, some of the sessions facilitate the release of perhaps unnecessary bonds. The messages from the deceased include suggestions to go on with life; they may bring closure to a worry held by the participant, they can release from guilt, and they can give explanations of family issues that are revelations to the participant. They often move the participants along the path to their own lives, but without severing a relationship. What strikes me as amazing about these sessions is that the spiritual guidance that comes is not something that the facilitators or I could have predicted, but something that emerges from the actual situation of the bereaved and the deceased.

Irene Blinston's Facilitation

The following stories come from people who have been working closely with me in this research, and have been through the process themselves and are members of the facilitation team. Irene shares an experience of guiding someone through the psychomanteum. Steven shares his own experience of going through the process.

Irene Blinston

I think my most profound experience with an actual client was a person whose daughter was her soul connection, the joy of her life. Her daughter was killed in a car accident in another state. This woman was grieving so heavily for ten months that her therapist, who knew about our research, asked her if she would consider coming, and she did.

She cried through the whole pre-interview, went through an entire box of tissues, showed me several pictures, and spoke in great pain about her daughter. I put her in the psychomanteum. We sit outside in meditation, holding the space for each person who goes through.

After about forty five minutes, I will usually go up to the door, open it gently, and ask them if they are done or if they would like more time. As I was approaching the door like I normally do, I heard her cry out in pain, and then extreme sobbing, and I thought, "She needs more time." So I sat down. I thought, "I'm on a time schedule!" and she wouldn't stop sobbing. I thought, "Okay, I just have to trust that all is what it should be, and the timing will be right."

At the exact time I needed to have her be done, she stopped sobbing, and it was very quiet in the room. I went and got her and asked her to come in to talk with me. When we spoke afterward, she told me she had realized that the way she was connected to her daughter through this whole time after her death was through the pain that she felt for the loss. She told me her daughter had said very clearly, while she was in the psychomanteum, that they did not need to be connected by pain, because they were always connected by love. That was when she burst into tears.

After that experience, she was a transformed woman. Any tears that came to her were with a smile and a feeling of how connected she was to her daughter the whole time in love. I did see her again. She went through again, and her life has been completely transformed. I can't say it was completely by the psychomanteum experience, but certainly it had a great deal to do with some decisions that she then made in her life. It was one of the wonderful experiences that I had as companion on the journey.

Steven Schmitz

I want to share an experience I had myself in the psychomanteum. It is similar to the experiences of people I've facilitated going through who have had grief unresolved for a long period of time.

My story was that when I was really young I had a cousin, with whom I was very close, who died. In those days, they didn't talk a lot about death. Death was almost an embarrassment. I was just living my life like any normal young kid, and then I was told that she had died.

I was shocked because there was no preparation. There was no honoring of me and my feelings. I was told very abruptly, "She's dead. We're going to the funeral." I remember crying a lot.

For most of my life, when I've shared that story with people, I've come to tears. I couldn't speak without my voice cracking, without being emotional. Even in the first phase of the psychomanteum, in the discussion about my relationship with my cousin, I'm crying on the tape. I couldn't speak to the facilitator without my voice cracking and hesitating.

I went into the psychomanteum. It was very interesting because after only an hour of talking and about an hour of sitting alone, I felt my cousin's presence. It wasn't like a face or a ghost or a touch. It was just a form of energy. I felt this thing being pulled out of my chest. I thought my heart was going to be pulled out, but what I realized was that she was taking the grief out of my heart. I surrendered and let go, and it went away. I had a communication with her because I didn't get a chance to say good-bye or to talk to her about some things that I needed to finish with her.

At the end of that hour, I went into the debriefing, and there were no tears. The grief was gone because what I realized, and what she told me, is that part of the grief I was feeling was that I felt there was no longer a relationship. There was a sense of loss. What she conveyed to me was that the connection is always there. The connection was still there. It was a real letting go of that grief I had held onto for over forty years. Within a single process, I was able to let go of that, move on, and have my life transformed.

Research Results

We have now completed two series of studies with the psychomanteum bereavement process. Using a strict research protocol within the process, we have participants complete questionnaires before they go through the process, after the third stage, and one month later to check for the stability of the experience. With the bereavement check list, we ask participants to rate the level of twenty one bereavement effects, such as sadness, grief, guilt, thinking about the person every day, anger, love, and longing. A scale of one to seven lets them indicate the strength of the feeling. The changes in the ratings after completing the process show decreases or increases in the feelings that can be statistically analyzed. For example, in the first study with twenty seven participants, the most significant changes in the group average ratings were in the need to communicate, which dropped from 4.40 to 2.14, grief, which dropped from 2.88 to 1.59, and unresolved feelings, which dropped from 3.00 to 2.52. Nine of the twenty one changes were statistically significant (probability values ranged from 0.05 to 0.0008, Wilcoxon signed ranks test), and the others all showed shifts in the direction of resolution. In terms of individual changes, in the second group of one hundred participants, ninety two showed changes in the direction of healing. In the first series of twenty seven participants, thirteen felt they had a contact or connection with the deceased, and in second series of one hundred, just completed, sixty four persons reported a contact.

We have had people who are Christian ministers and people who are Buddhist practitioners, people in their twenties and people in their eighties. The process has benefited people who have had recent deaths in their lives and people for whom it has been more than forty years.

The psychomanteum process is obviously not for everyone, but seems to be a compassionate addition to the range of support for healing bereavement. All our participants were volunteers, and given the nature of the process, this is appropriate. The qualities our clients have in common are a readiness for change and an interest in trying the technique.

References

Arcangel, Diane. *Afterlife Encounters: Ordinary People, Extraordinary Experiences.* Charlottesville, VA: Hampton Roads, 2005.

Hastings, A., Hutton, M., Braud, W., Bennett, C., Berk, I., Boynton, T., Dawn, C., Ferguson, F., Goldman, A., Greene, E., Hewett, M., Lind, V., McLellan, K., Steinbach-Humphrey, S. 2002. Psychomanteum Research: Experiences and Effects on Bereavement. *Omega: Journal of Death and Dying, 45*(3), 195–212.

Klass, Dennis. Silverman, P. R., and Nickman, S. L. (Eds.). *Continuing Bonds: New U-Understandings of Grief.* New York: Taylor and Francis, 1996.

Moody, R. A. *Life after Life.* New York: Bantam, 1975.

Moody, Raymond. Family reunions: Visionary encounters with the departed in a modern-day psychomanteum. *Journal of Near-Death Studies,* 1992, *11*(2), 83–121.

Moody, Raymond, with Perry, P. *Reunions: Visionary Encounters with Departed Loved Ones.* New York: Ivy Books, 1993.

Radin, Dean, and Rebman, Jeanne. "Are Phantasms Fact or Fantasy? A Preliminary Investigation of Apparitions Evoked in the Laboratory." *Journal of the Society for Psychical Research, 61*(843), 1996, 65–87.

Roll, William. G. "Psychomanteum Research: A Pilot Study." *Journal of Near Death Studies, 22*(4), 2003, 251–260.

Suedfeld, P., and Borrie, R. A. "Health and Therapeutic Applications of Chamber and Flotation Restricted Environmental Stimulation Therapy (REST)." *Psychology and Health,* 14, 1999, 545–566.

GROUP SPIRITUAL DIRECTION

Now we examine the work of group spiritual guidance. Janice Farrell outlines the importance of authenticity, deep listening, and honesty in developing a spiritual guidance group into a spiritual community. She writes of the process of sitting together in silence, emptying oneself, and allowing new and often surprising insights to emerge.

Liz Ellmann discusses her pioneering work with spiritual guidance groups in corporations. She brings a group of businesspeople together in a corporate conference room. They generally begin by discussing an inspirational book, but after a few sessions, the book becomes less relevant as they begin to work with deep personal questions like, "Why did you choose your work?"; "What are your hopes?"; and "How come you're still here?"; "What happens if you leave?"

Genie Palmer stresses basic elements in her own approach to spiritual guidance group work. The first is mindfulness and being present. As members consciously create a group circle they are called to bring Spirit to the center of the circle. The second is ritual. Groups begin with a simple ritual. Members create an altar for the center of the circle with sacred objects from their own traditions and life histories. The groups also work with the process of sitting in council, a practice rooted in Native American traditions. The group uses a talking stick, which is held by whomever is speaking. This helps the group to remember the sacredness of speaking in the circle and to honor each speaker with contemplative listening. Another important element in the spiritual guidance groups is silence. As Genie puts it, "Silence gives us the opportunity to hear the real Director."

Developing Spiritual Community in Group Spiritual Direction

I fell in love with group methods way back in the sixties. When I was in a group dynamic course at San Francisco State, all hell was breaking loose — it was the Haight Ashbury, the experimental college, the anti-war movement. Half of the students in my class were picked to sit in a group that was an encounter group with no rules. The other half were picked to sit behind the one-way mirror and watch as the group developed. I happened to be picked for the group behind the mirror.

I remember the fun we had in the common restroom, because we knew Joe and Sally intimately, but they had no idea who we were. We'd start a conversation, and they'd look at us like, "Who are you?" We were enjoying the strange new dynamic we were seeing.

But all jokes aside, that class started my real love affair with the incredible beauty of human persons coming together and beginning to share the depth of their joy and their pain in a group setting.

I, for one, have always felt that group spiritual direction was like listening to and being in a jazz combo. It is what attracts me so deeply and what continues to fill me with joy as I work with groups. There is a sense that we drop our agendas, that we drop the mind, that we become so mindful that we're mindless, that we sit with each other, and see that light speaking to the Source in each of us. It's as though we are all listening to the One who orchestrates this incredible jazz. When we let go, we enter spontaneous, impromptu beauty.

When we sit in a group, if we really listen we can hear the music of each other. This is not to say that there are no conflicts, differences, and disagreements. But what we need to do is simply to sit and feel reverence for those differences, to see and experience the God-self in each of us. A wise sage once said, "We will never have peace until we can each really see God in each other and show reverence no matter what our differences are."

How timely it is that pioneering work in group spiritual direction continues today when we so desperately need it! What would our world be like if we dropped our agendas and came together, all of us, in webs of consciousness? What would happen if we sat and opened to the Source of Life and asked that we be filled with wisdom? What if we decided to speak and lead each other from that wise Source of our shared being?

It is with great joy that I speak about some of the very beautiful similarities and differences between one-on-one direction and group guidance. Although many characteristics are the same, there are characteristics that are particular to individual spiritual guidance and others particular to group spiritual direction. But before I even get to that, I'd like to note that groups don't all look the same. There are interesting similarities between types of groups. Spiritual direction groups, no matter what incarnation, share certain values.

For instance, Peter Senge, the corporate psychologist, wrote a marvelous book in the late eighties called *The Fifth Discipline*. He spoke about bringing corporate groups together and asking the participants to drop their agendas, to empty, to rest, and to speak out of their deep selves in order to find the wisdom that could lead those corporations forward in more humane and socially conscious ways.

Another example is Charles Garfield, the transpersonal psychologist who created Shanti, the Berkeley, California, program for people who were counseling the dying. He wrote a book called *Wisdom Circles*. It was about coming into presence with each other. It was about dropping the preconceived mental images, judgments, and worries, and truly being present.

Again and again, spiritual direction groups will exemplify these characteristics: coming together with presence, coming together with mindfulness, coming together for discernment, and coming together with an appreciation of differences. So no matter what language we use, we're talking about something that we so desperately need in our time.

Let me focus a little more specifically now on some of the group spiritual guidance characteristics. Often what is said is that when people gather for group spiritual guidance, the necessary mindset includes a willingness to be authentic in your spiritual journey, where you are now, and willingness to come together authentically and intentionally for that purpose. Another essential component is a willingness to listen to each other, to wholeheartedly participate with the other, to share, and to be open and responsive.

Groups need people who are willing to be honest and open in their own sharing. When people do that intentionally, there is the creation of a small true community where there is reciprocity, where there is mutuality of sharing. A group like this intentionally roots itself in the Source. In a very real sense, the group intentionally says, "I am aware of the presence of God," pledging to each other to pay attention to the movements of God in the group.

Briefly, I will now discuss the similarities between group spiritual guidance and one-on-one spiritual guidance. As in one-on-one spiritual guidance, for most of us who are facilitating group spiritual guidance groups we share the sense that the real director, the real guide, is not our ego-driven and circumscribed self but the Source of wisdom. In such a group, we literally can lean back into God. The approach we take is contemplative rather than problem solving. By contemplative, I mean "the long loving look at the real." The long loving look at the real is that moment in which we are not attempting to fix the other. We are not attempting to solve the problem, but to be present and receptive, to be that concave being for the other.

In groups, the content, as in one-on-one direction, may be focused on any facet of our lives. It could be the experience of getting a parking ticket! It might be the experience of getting caught in the rain and being drenched! If we stay long enough with any human experience, it can be a gateway into the mystery of God, into the mystery of the Divine. In group spiritual guidance, as in one-on-one spiritual direction, the focus is on that movement, that stirring, that response of the Divine within your life.

It is very important that the actual nature of the sharing in groups, as in one-on-one spiritual guidance, be dialogic. This dynamic is not one person telling another, but both persons or all in a group listening. The word "dialogue," *dialogos*, means the word, the logos, or the meaning coming through. When we really listen to each other, we are not planning what we're going to say next. Ideally, this is what we do in one-on-one spiritual guidance sessions. If we do this kind of listening in a group, the same thing happens. There is a creative upwelling in the conversation: co-creative wisdom is shared. Of course, as in one-on-one spiritual guidance, group spiritual guidance also has a safety container that everything that is shared is confidential and not to be shared outside the group.

But now we will turn to some of the distinctive characteristics of group spiritual guidance. This is the most exciting part. In group spiritual guidance one of the most important aspects of the experience is that when people come together, there is an extended time for silence, an extended period of time to let oneself be in the presence of the holy as an individual but also as a group. There is an incredible self-emptying. The previous agendas, the ideas about where this group could go, in fact any goal orientation gets dropped and there is openness to the presence and guidance of the Holy One.

What happens? Surprises happen! Often in the sharing, what happens is a palpable experience of the Presence. When it is shared, it totally breaks open our own narrow images or senses of who the Divine is. I always remember a young man in one of the groups that I facilitated at Mercy Center who was very wild looking. He was younger than everyone else. We were all middle-aged and better. He was in his thirties, with wild hair and different kinds of clothes. He always had incredibly creative ideas. We all loved him. Halfway through the program he said to that group, "You know, I've been in the quiet now for fifteen minutes and I keep being nudged. I finally heard what it was that God wanted me to know." We were all at the edge of our seats waiting, and he said, "God said to me, 'You're not wild enough!'" We all just burst out laughing!

It's true that there is this incredible playfulness, spontaneity, wildness, joy, and depth that none of us alone could ever hear about were we not privileged and graced to be in the company of others who are having a different experience of the Divine. It whets the appetite for more and more and more. For those of us who offer one-on-one direction, the privilege of being in groups is exactly that. It is such a privilege being able, in a group, to experience the wildness, the beauty, the joy of God, the depth of God's lovingness and wisdom.

Spiritual Guidance in the Boardroom

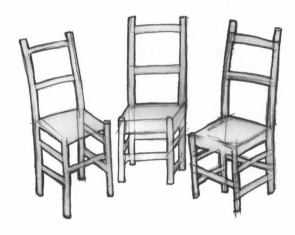

When I entered divinity school, I felt called, I thought, to be a leader in a church building. I had been in a corporate environment, and thought I just needed to switch. Now I take the experience that I had in corporate life and bring the ministry back into the workplace. I do a form of group spiritual guidance with corporate groups, and what follows are real examples from my experience.

You can model one-on-one spiritual direction with two chairs. There is a sense of two human beings coming together, a spiritual director and a spiritual directee, a guide and someone looking for guidance, a seeker and a teacher. But there is also always a third chair in spiritual direction, and that third chair is the Divine.

A spiritual guide is aware that there is a third presence, the true director, the one that is setting the compass course. The opportunity for spiritual knowledge becomes richer as you add more chairs to the circle.

As the facilitator of group spiritual direction, our role is to encourage the articulation and make explicit of the experience of the divine. This happens now in many religious settings: at spirituality centers, at churches, and in synagogues. There really is a bursting forth of group spiritual direction happening in spiritual buildings.

What I wanted to experiment with is what happens if we take a corporate conference room and set up the chairs like we might in a church or religious building, and invite there to be contemplation and silence.

Of course, as we become more awake, we begin to realize that the corporate buildings are not secular at all. The work that is being done in the corporate buildings is also incredibly sacred. It is a privilege to walk with groups of corporate people who are struggling to make meaning of their work in a spiritual context.

Let me backtrack to how I got started in this work. In my twenties, I worked on Wall Street as a trader. I went dutifully to church, and I use "dutifully" because I have always been involved in spiritual community where I have lived. I was asked to serve on the finance committee at the Riverside Church in Manhattan, and I did that by taking my corporate knowledge and helping out the church.

I noticed in my trading life that there was a growing cognitive dissonance about integration of my spiritual life. I was thinking, "Now, I'm taking these corporate tools and helping my church understand its finances, but what is the church giving me to help me make sense out of my corporate life?" That was very puzzling to me. It was so puzzling to me, in fact, that after six or seven years of trading, I started seeing a therapist about it. In therapy I was asking, "How is it that I've arrived at this American dream—I have a wonderful partner, I have a home and a great job, and I'm going to church and I'm being a good servant at church-but I'm not feeling spirituality nourished?" It just wasn't working for me.

My dear therapist said, "Stay with that. What would it be like for you to imagine yourself not trading, not a vice president, not living with the responsibilities of leading on a trading floor? What would that be like?"

I couldn't wrap my mind around that. She invited me to consider Moses' struggle of being called out into the desert and having to let go and lead people God only knows where. I stayed with that long enough until I had the courage to cut the cord from mother banker's trust and step out into uncharted territory for me. It was very lonely, very hard, and very confusing for an ego that had its life all figured out not too many months previous.

I was not grateful at the time. I was very confused. After years of study and travel to India and Thailand and Sri Lanka, I found the true journey for me was to go deeper into the spiritual teachings of certain texts, and then bring the wisdom of those texts back to circles of people in the workplace. I finally discovered that there might be integration of spirituality and work.

Some people have said, "How do you find your way into a corporation to offer this kind of program?" My answer is just that it has been very serendipitous and totally by grace. It's all about saying "I'm feeling called to do corporate spirituality." I said it in my church community, in my friend community, and in the grocery store.

If I'm feeling called to something, I can say that I'm passionate about it. What has happened time and time again is an attorney will say, "You know, I have the same desire to make some sense out of my law practice and my creative practice and my spiritual life. We have a conference room across the hall. Why don't you come in?" A church that was looking for a way to help its youth integrate spirituality with their work life invited me through one of its members to come into a brokerage house. It felt like, "Oh, here is God truly laughing at me." I walked by all of the computer screens, all of the screamers and yellers, and went into the corporate board room. There I gathered people together to talk about what was meaningful for them in their spiritual life, in their work life, and how they might come together.

In addition to bringing spirituality to a workplace, dealing with tragedy is another role of a group spiritual director. I got a call on September, 12, 2001, from someone who worked in a government agency. I had written an article in *Presence*, the journal of Spiritual

Directors International. The article was about corporate spirituality. The woman calling me had read it in a spirituality center a couple of weeks earlier. She was now faced with her staff, who had watched the burning of the Pentagon across the street. No one wanted to be in their conference room any more because there was such a sense of grief and loss there. She was in Washington, D.C.; I live in Seattle. She said, "Would you coach me in how to bring a new understanding of what we are as a team now, in the midst of this, and will you help me transform the conference room as you've been transforming conference rooms in Seattle?" It was an incredible privilege to walk with her and her group in spiritual direction. We made new meaning of the experience they had all lived through, and would continue living through.

An executive director of a large national not-for-profit called the Spiritual Directors International office saying that their volunteer coordinator had been hit by a bus and died. The caller was asking Spiritual Directors International for a spiritual director to come into her work place and be with the community as it processed the loss of this twenty-seven-year old woman. I helped her find a spiritual director, because it is now my role to help seekers connect with spiritual directors. I helped find a spiritual director to come in and work with the staff and volunteers who had to make sense out of the tragedy of this young person dying.

When I was at the Parliament of World Religions one summer, I learned something about the Hindu tradition. A new member of Spiritual Directors International told me that in India work is worship. She finds it so confusing when she comes to visit the West that we have this split: work is in one corner and spirituality is in another. In her Bombay culture, going to work is giving back to God, giving back to that which is holy, giving back to the source of life, giving back to the source of creativity. I raise that issue because I think that is one of the ways, as facilitators of group spiritual direction, that we can assist people in their search for integration. We can plant some different ways of looking at our work so it is not competing with worship.

It's actually a form of worship. It's a form of giving back in service to our world. Doing spiritual guidance in a corporate setting requires a certain amount of creative thinking. Although corporate groups are still groups, they have certain needs and can be helped by awareness of their specific situation.

One of the ways to bring corporate people together is to have a text that we read together. This is more a marketing ploy, but it has been very, very helpful. I don't go to the group and say, "Would you like to be a part of group spiritual direction for twelve weeks in this conference room where we're going to transform the workplace?" That doesn't work very well. What has worked is to use books such as *The Artist's Way at Work* by Julia Cameron. The book has a nice twelve-week flow to it. It gives you credibility. It gives a safe framework to start with. My experience is we start with it, but the book is gone by about session three. Really what is happening in the group is spiritual direction. Each participant starts sharing feelings: "You know, in the last week I've been trying, experimenting with five minutes of silence in the morning, and it's so hard!" or "I'm finding great joy," or "My child wants to participate in this with me. Is that a good idea? Is that not a good idea?" All of a sudden, there is a tremendous amount of shared wisdom that happens in the circle.

Another reason I find Cameron's book to be so helpful is she names the soaring experience of spirituality without using "spirituality" until about Essay Six. She writes about the abyss quality of purposing a spiritual path. That "soaring" and "abyss" naming helps working people name the shifting that is happening for them. Another author worth using is Parker Palmer. Palmer wrote a beautiful book called *The Active Life: A Spirituality of Work, Creativity, and Caring*. He also wrote *Let Your Life Speak*. He is a master teacher, and his books have short essays that allow the mind of a working person to be engaged with the material, then drop into the silence. His books foster the spiritual delving that happens in group spiritual direction. Twelve weeks in a corporate, banker's, or hospital's mindset is a quarter. I say, "Give me from January to March. It's just an experiment." I think it is important to have a time frame. It should be a time period that is long enough for there to be intimacy grown, and short enough that someone can go on with their life and be integrated in new and different ways.

Once a week and for an hour, we gather in their conference room. I want them in the heart of downtown. I want it to be on their floor, just across the hall, in their own conference room. The time and place to meet need to be super easy. The session needs to be in the time frame of a working person, which is about an hour. Cusps of the day are very good times. Setting the time from seven to eight in the morning or from four thirty to five thirty in the evening, right when people are either on their way in or on their way out, makes it easy for them to get there.

Usually people come to work with some aspiration that they've lost touch with. Group spiritual direction in the workplace has been a lot about helping people remember what attracted them to the Environmental Protection Agency, what attracted them to becoming a lawyer and help fight the injustices of the world, what attracted them to Providence Health Care and wanting to heal people.

The group moves toward refining their understanding of their place in the work and their aspiration, what attracted them to begin with. That discovery is very much a part of what I've witnessed in the group spiritual direction process.

Very simple questions like, "Why did you choose your work?"; "How come you're still here?"; "What are your hopes?"; "What are you afraid of in leaving?"; "What happens if you leave?"; and "What happens if you stay?" are questions that the holy holds so well in a corporate setting.

I remember one participant saying, "No wonder we have boring ideas around here. Look at these grey walls!" So what we would do each week is create a vibrant place: light a candle, bring in some chairs, or create a centerpiece that helped to inspire something beyond the grey walls and the square table that we meet around. Changing the structure and organization of their corporate space is also a modeling of possibility for spiritual change.

I will end with one small piece of advice for those who may begin doing their own form of spiritual guidance in the boardroom: begin and end with silence. Silence is something we are so starved for in the workplace. The guide has a gift, a power to invite a room of people to shared silence. Give them permission to slow down and be silent, so they can spend an hour in a new, deeper awareness together.

 ## References

Bryan, Mark with Cameron, Julia and Allen, Catherine. *The Artist's Way at Work: Riding the Dragon.* New York: William Morrow, 1998.

Palmer, Parker J. *The Active Life: A Spirituality of Work, Creativity, and Caring.* San Francisco: Jossey-Bass, 1990.

Palmer, Parker J. *Let Your Life Speak: Listening for the Voice of Vocation.* San Francisco: Jossey-Bass, 2000.

The Process of Group Spiritual Guidance

I feel a great sense of passion for the pioneering work that we do in group spiritual guidance and direction. During the educational process of getting a masters degree in gerontology, I took a minor in counseling. I became very connected with the classes in small group behavior. It was there I began to learn some things about group behavior and group dynamics. Those classes stirred up my passion for group work, and from that point on, I've vacillated to be either part of a group, starting a group, getting a group together, herding a group, shepherding a group, and so on. In fact, when I look back on thirty years of nursing prior to this new work, I realize that I have been doing group spiritual guidance for years, and years, and years. It has been called something different each time.

One thing I can say from my years of experience is that there is still a lot of confusion with spirituality and religion. As contemporary spiritual guides and directors, we have the potential to move people beyond their narrow limits and their rigid beliefs, to help them look at spirituality and life differently. We have the possibility of helping people live more in terms of soul and spirit. We can bring them to their own potential for growth, change, and transformation. Our work is helping people make wiser and better choices.

Currently, I teach group spiritual guidance, which is part of the spiritual guidance program at the Institute for Transpersonal Psychology. The students go through a year-long practicum in which they learn and practice very practical skills. The third quarter of the year-long practicum is now devoted to group spiritual guidance. I find that combining aspects of transpersonal psychology with various forms of group process has allowed me to create a form of group guidance that nurtures whole-person spirituality.

What continually amazes me about spiritual guidance, and particularly group guidance, is the sense of mystery that is always present in a group. It is present in one-on-one guidance, but for whatever reason, it seems to be much more present for me within a group. There is something special about the energy and the dynamics that come together in a group. Spirit is always present in a group. In fact, the presence of that mystery may be one of the most important aspects of group guidance.

Christina Baldwin has written a book called *Calling the Circle*. She says, "When people live in a culture that has forgotten its relationship to mystery, a number of things go awry." [35] We've seen that happen enough in today's world. Baldwin notes that "We cease to regard life as sacred because we don't hear it described this way. We forget we are the sisters and brothers of all life because we are told we are the 'masters' of creation. We revel in fantasies of specialness, and are tormented by our sense of isolation. And having lost our understanding that center serves as our point of interaction with the sacred, we fill the hole with substitutions." In today's world, some of these substitutions are excesses of food, drugs, alcohol, sex, and materialism, along with status, personal power, racial hatred, and violence. Baldwin reminds us that indigenous people have a common element of coming together and sharing sacred center. They have not forgotten. Perhaps we need to study their sacred ways and bring their rituals back into our lives.

Group spiritual guidance in particular offers us the opportunity to return to a sacred center, and to fill that center with things that nourish our soul and help us keep the mystery alive. In a group, we have the opportunity to share vulnerable aspects of ourselves on our spiritual journey. Perhaps for some people in the group, it is the first time they've had the chance to share such experiences. Sharing in the group also gives us the opportunity to find meaning and purpose in our life experiences, both the traumatic experiences and the exceptional experiences, and find a way to hold both without necessarily getting lost in either.

In the group we have a conscious allowance of spirit to be present. It is the influence of spirit that creates potential for change and transformation. In his book *Everything Belongs*, noted spiritual director and Franciscan priest Richard Rohr declares that "We cannot attain the presence of God because we're already totally in the presence of God."[36] We're just not aware of it. Group spiritual guidance allows us an opportunity to bring spirit back in and to become aware. As we become more aware of the spiritual and transpersonal dimensions, our values and our behaviors begin to change.

Transpersonal psychology, like spiritual guidance, defies being pinned down by any one particular definition. While transpersonal psychology has been around for thirty years or so, spiritual direction has been around for centuries and centuries. Yet both are evolving fields. Even so, for many people out there in the world, both of these fields remain very misunderstood. As spiritual guides and especially in group spiritual direction, we can help people understand that better.

Spiritual guidance and transpersonal psychology have much to offer each other. Spiritual guidance provides us with a useful container in which to apply the transpersonal principles as personal values and bring those values into the lives of ordinary people in everyday life. Transpersonal psychology, on the other hand, offers spiritual guidance the opportunity to be more inclusive, more integrative, to address the more that we are and that we can be. Bringing together transpersonal psychology and spiritual guidance, therefore, strengthens the bridge between psychology and spirituality.

I want to point out some specific aspects of the model of group spiritual guidance that I use at ITP. We rely heavily on Rose Mary Dougherty's model as presented in her book, *Group Spiritual Direction: Community for Discernment*, as a foundational model of group spiritual guidance. She is the pioneer in the field. She points us in the direction of the importance of community, and how this kind of guidance helps us develop that community. In her book on group spiritual guidance, Dougherty provides this useful African proverb: "It is because one antelope will blow the dust from the other's eye that the two antelopes walk together."[37] This proverb aptly describes the process of discernment that takes place in all spiritual guidance, whether it is individual or group spiritual guidance.

Dougherty goes on to explain that in the group we become guides and directors for each member in the group. Through this interceding presence of the group, the dust is blown from our eyes and then we can see clearly. We can see the presence of spirit. We can become more aware. With that as our foundation, I will discuss four main aspects of the type of group spiritual guidance that I teach the students at ITP.

The first one is the aspect of mindfulness. This topic has been endlessly discussed, but mindfulness and being present are so important when a group comes together, and when we sit in a circle and find ways to reveal aspects of our self. When we create our mindful, intentional circle, we do so consciously knowing that we're bringing spirit back to the center of the circle. A circle represents that wholeness and that holiness that we are all seeking. Christina Baldwin tells us that a circle is not about rearranging the chairs in a certain way, but it is about coming together and doing things differently from the way we're normally accustomed to doing things. The circle is a symbol of being and doing differently. Actually creating a circle with the group is a physical reminder of that value. A circle of chairs invites us to be more inclusive and more integrative.

The second important aspect that I teach the students is the importance of ritual. We always start our group work with ritual. A very important part of the ritual that we do is the creation of altars. Each student in the group is invited to create an altar out of their own spiritual tradition, religious tradition, perhaps their culture, perhaps around relationship.

In bringing together the various parts of an altar, which may include a number of sacred objects, the students are allowed the opportunity to share part of their tradition with the group. They may bring in pieces from another country. They may bring in important parts of their family history. What's very interesting is that there is always somebody in the group that prepares an altar from a tradition that someone else in the group has not experienced before. The altars are not only educational, but they allow for further group guidance. In one class, a student brought in some wonderful objects from a Navaho tribe. These were some very sacred objects, and we also did some drumming and chanting.

Another time two women in our group who were Jewish brought in altar objects from their tradition, and they also brought in a mini seder supper because it was the time of their Passover celebration. They wanted to share that experience with their ITP family, with their classmates. The special dinner was a wonderful opportunity for many of us who had not experienced that tradition to be in community with them. The altars have become the heart of our group spiritual guidance because they allow the students to sit with one another in a new awareness.

It is important to remember that you can't sit in a group like that without pushing all sorts of buttons. When you bring in an altar from particular traditions, in which there are sacred objects and important family things, all your spiritual issues come up. Oftentimes, group members have an uncomfortable feeling sitting with a tradition that they grew up with and then left. They may want nothing to do with the tradition anymore, but sure enough, they'll sit in the group right next to the person who's going to do a whole ritual about that tradition.

The group invites them to sit with that, to notice what's uncomfortable, what gets triggered, and what comes up. That becomes part of our group spiritual guidance process. The student gets to share, in the moment, both their inspirations and their spiritual pain. Religious issues or family of origin issues come up because of objects on their altar. What started out as a simple ritual to begin group guidance has become an important part of the fabric of that process.

A third aspect of our teaching at ITP is that we sit in council. This is also an important part of many Native American cultures. Part of sitting in council is the use of a talking stick. We often use a formal talking stick, but we have also used special stones, rocks, and pieces of wood that have been brought in from the forest. The talking stick sits alongside the altar and becomes part of the process. No one talks in the group unless they are holding the talking stick. Holding the talking stick creates acknowledgement of that person. The talking stick is a way to honor the person who is speaking from the heart. The talking stick helps the group remember the sacred by remembering the person who is speaking.

When we sit in council there is no cross talk. As long as a person is holding the talking stick, they are the speaker. The group's task is to provide deep and holy listening while that person is holding the stick.

The fourth and final aspect I will discuss here is silence. One of the greatest aspects of group spiritual guidance is the opportunity to sit in silence with a group of people, particularly if it's not always comfortable. There is so much learning that comes from that spiritual practice. In silence we are able to listen more deeply, to hear the still, small voice that is speaking to us and through us. Silence gives us the opportunity to hear the real Director.

Group spiritual guidance is a continual process of learning to let go and surrender. There are really no goals to group spiritual guidance. It's not about resolutions. It's not about finding answers, although that often occurs. It's more about the "sitting with." Group spiritual guidance is more about being with one another in a way that is so different from how we show up generally in the world. It's learning to be mindful not only of ourselves but of other people. We become mindful that there is a great presence working through us.

In this process, we come to know compassion in action, and we discover an appreciation for each other's unique differences as well as our similarities. My intention here has been to show you how transpersonal psychology and spiritual guidance are natural complements to each other and how they share some similarities. One of the most important similarities is that they share the capacity to be in the mystery.

I will conclude with some words of wisdom from Christina Baldwin's book, *Calling the Circle*,[38] that, for me, go right to the heart of this kind of group spiritual guidance:

Come. Come sit with me on this boulder. We will take turns boring the auger into stone. It is not such hard work when more than one is working. We will tell each other stories. We will help each other do the tasks of our lives. We will wear this stone away without violence. There has been enough violence.

We will talk to the granite.
We will not give up.
We will be like drops of water falling on a stone. . .

References

Baldwin, Christina. *Calling the Circle: The First and Future Culture*. New York: Bantam, 1994, 1998.

Dougherty, Rose Mary. *Group Spiritual Direction: Community for Discernment*. Mahweh, NJ: Paulist Press, 1995.

Rohr, Richard. *Everything Belongs: The Gift of Contemplative Prayer*. New York: Crossroad, 1999, 2003.

Wilson, Andrew, ed. *World Scripture: A Comparative Anthology of Sacred Texts*. St. Paul, MN: Paragon House, 1991.

Notes

Introduction

1. Abraham Maslow, *Toward a Psychology of Being,* 206

2. This discussion is based on a description of transpersonal psychology by Robert Hutchins, Ph.D., an early graduate of the Institute of Transpersonal Psychology.

3. Please see R. Valle, "The Emergence of Transpersonal Psychology" in *Existential-Phenomenological Perspectives in Psychology.*

1. Reflections on the Spiritual Path

4. John 3:8, NRSV

3. Spiritual Intimacy

5. Song of Songs 1:4a, NRSV

4. Spiritual Guidance in the Sufi Tradition

6. Fadiman and Frager, *Essential Sufism,* 244.

7. Fadiman and Frager, *Essential Sufism,* 244.

5. Four Principles in Spiritual Guidance

8. Daniel J. Ladinsky, *Love Poems from God,* 191.

8. Spiritual Direction and Mystical Experience

9. Henri Nouwen, *Sabbatical Journey,* 5–6.

9. Breakthroughs in Spiritual Guidance

10. Luke 18:17, NRSV

11. Arthur Green, Nahman of Bratslav quoted in, *Tormented Master*, 310.

12. Louis J. Puhl, S.J. (tr.), *The Spiritual Exercises of St. Ignatius*, (Westminster, MD: Newman Press, 1963), p. 147.

13. Reiner Schurmann, *Meister Eckhart* (Bloomington: Indiana University Press, 1978), p. xiv.

10. Spiritual Guidance on the Margins of Society

14. Wisdom of Solomon 7:27, NRSV.

11. Spiritual Guidance at the End of Life

15. See Margaret Guenther, "Companions at the Threshold: Spiritual Direction with the Dying," 30, and also see Thomas Merton, "Thomas Merton on Spiritual Direction," 41.

16. Sri Aurobindo, *The Synthesis of Yoga*, 47.

17. Sri Aurobindo, *The Essential Aurobindo*, 39.

18. Sri Aurobindo, *The Synthesis of Yoga*, 53.

19. Sri Aurobindo, *The Synthesis of Yoga*, 52.

20. Sri Aurobindo, *Integral Yoga: Sri Aurobindo's Teaching and Method of Practice*, 101.

21. Sri Aurobindo, *The Synthesis of Yoga*, 55–56.

22. Sri Aurobindo, *The Synthesis of Yoga*, 60.

23. Sri Aurobindo, *The Synthesis of Yoga*, 592.

24. Sri Aurobindo, Integral Yoga: Sri Aurobindo's Method and Teaching of Practice, 159.

25. Sri Aurobindo, *The Synthesis of Yoga*, 523.

26. Sri Aurobindo, *The Synthesis of Yoga*, 56.

27. Sri Aurobindo, *The Synthesis of Yoga*, 49.

28. Sri Aurobindo, *The Synthesis of Yoga*, 60.

29. Sogyal Rinpoche, *The Tibetan Book of Living and Dying*, 214–216.

12. A New Approach to Grief Work

30. Hastings, et al., "Psychomanteum Research: Experiences and Effects on Bereavement," 195–212.

31. See his discussion of this phenomenon in his book, *Life after Life*.

32. See Diane Arcangel, *Afterlife Encounters: Ordinary People, Extraordinary Experiences*; and Hastings, et al., "Psychomanteum Research: Experiences and Effects on Bereavement;" and Raymond Moody, "Family Reunions: Visionary Encounters with the Departed in a Modern-day Psychomanteum;" and Dean Radin & Jeanne Rebman, "Are Phantasms Fact or Fantasy?" and William G. Roll, "Psychomanteum Research: A Pilot Study."

33. See Suedfeld and R. A. Borrie, "Health and Therapeutic Applications of Chamber and Flotation Restricted Environmental Stimulation Therapy (REST)."

34. See Dennis Klass and R. Silverman and S. L. Nickman, (Eds.). *Continuing Bonds: New U-Understandings of Grief*.

15. The Process of Group Spiritual Guidance

35. Christina Baldwin, *Calling the Circle*, xiii.

36. Richard Rohr, *Everything Belongs*, 29.

37. Andrew Wilson, ed., *World Scripture: A Comparative Anthology of Sacred Texts*, 187, is quoted in Rose Mary Dougherty, *Group Spiritual Direction*, 24.

38. Christina Baldwin, *Calling the Circle*, 11.

Contributor Biographies

Liz Budd Ellmann, M.Div., is the Executive Director of Spiritual Directors International. Before joining Spiritual Directions International, she founded SoulTenders, a multifaith organization dedicated to tending the spirit of working people through the teaching and support of spiritual practices in the workplace. Liz earned a BA from Stanford University and a Master of Divinity degree from the Jesuit Seattle University.

Janice B. Farrell M.A., is a spiritual director, teacher and supervisor of spiritual directors, retreat director, workshop facilitator, and Mercy Center adjunct staff member. She holds an MA in humanistic and transpersonal psychology and received postgraduate training and state certification as a holistic health educator and counselor, and received postgraduate work in contemporary theology at the Graduate Theological Union in Berkeley, California.

Robert Frager, Ph.D., received his doctorate in Social Psychology from Harvard University. He has taught psychology at Harvard University, U.C. Berkeley, and U.C. Santa Cruz. He is the founder of the Institute of Transpersonal Psychology in Palo Alto, California and is presently Professor of Psychology and Director of the ITP Spiritual Guidance Program. He is the co-author of *Personality and Personality Growth* (6th edition, Prentice-Hall) and a variety of books and articles on psychology. He is a spiritual teacher and guide in the Sufi tradition and is the author of four books on Sufism and Islam: *Essential Sufism; Love is the Wine; Heart, Self and Soul;* and *The Wisdom of Islam.*

Gerald Hair Ph.D., has practiced spiritual direction and pastoral counseling for thirty six years. He was a Jesuit for twenty-five years, and founded the academic counseling department at Xavier University, Cincinnati and co-founded the Jesuit Renewal Center in Milford, Ohio, where he served as pastoral counselor, spiritual director, retreat director and teacher of spirituality for twelve years.

Arthur Hastings Ph.D., is Professor of Psychology and Director of the William James Center for Consciousness Studies at the Institute of Transpersonal Psychology. He received his doctorate in communications from Northwestern University and taught at Stanford University before coming to ITP. His publications include *With the Tongues of Men and Angels: A Study of Channeling.*

Robert H. Hopcke, M.A., MFT, has worked as a licensed Marriage and Family Therapist since 1986. He holds an M.A. in Theology in Pastoral Counseling from Pacific Lutheran Theological Seminary and an M.S. in Clinical Counseling from California State University. He was trained in spiritual direction at Mercy Center in Burlingame, California. His books include the best-seller *There Are No Accidents: Synchronicity and the Stories of Our Lives* and the *Guided Tour to the Collected Works of C.G. Jung,* which has become a standard introduction to Jung in colleges and universities. He currently works as a volunteer spiritual director for the Roman Catholic Archdiocese of San Francisco's Detention Ministry and is the co-coordinator of the Peace and Social Justice Group at his parish, Most Holy Redeemer, in San Francisco.

James Neafsey, D. Min., has been a spiritual director, retreat leader and teacher of Christian Spirituality for over thirty years. Jim received a Masters of Divinity from Weston School of Theology and a Doctor of Ministry in Art and Spirituality from the Graduate Theological Union. For the past thirteen years he has been a staff member and supervisor in several spiritual direction programs: Mercy Center in Burlingame,

California; Bread of Life Center in Davis, California; San Francisco Theological Seminary; and the Hawaii Program for the formation of Spiritual Directors. He teaches courses on discernment, prayer, and Christian mysticism in the graduate program for Pastoral Ministries at Santa Clara University.

Fr. Sean Olaoire, Ph.D., is a Catholic priest. Born in Ireland, he was holds a B.Sc. degree from the National University of Ireland. He is multilingual and holds an M.A. and Ph.D. in transpersonal psychology, and is a licensed clinical psychologist. He is cofounder and spiritual director of Companions on the Journey, an association of San Francisco Bay Area Catholics who are attempting to find "a new way of being truly Catholic."

Genie Palmer, Ph.D., is core faculty member and dissertation director at the Institute of Transpersonal Psychology. She is a member of the ITP Spiritual Guidance Council and has supervised ITP students in spiritual guidance and teaches group spiritual guidance in the ITP spiritual guidance practicum program.

Paul Roy, Ph.D., is Vice President for Academic Affairs of the Institute of Transpersonal Psychology. He also maintains a private practice as a clinical psychologist and as a spiritual director. He was Assistant Professor of Pastoral Counseling at the Weston Jesuit School of Theology in Cambridge, Massachusetts. Paul has over thirty years experience as a spiritual director.

Rabbi Zalman Schachter-Shalomi D.H.L., holds the World Wisdom Seat at Naropa University and is Professor Emeritus at Temple University. He is a major figure in the Jewish spiritual renewal movement. Reb Zalman was ordained in 1947 and received a D.H.L (Doctor of Hebrew Letters) in 1968 from Hebrew Union College. In 1989 Reb Zalman founded the Spiritual Eldering Institute. He has published over one hundred fifty articles and monographs on the

Jewish spiritual life, and has translated many Hassidic and Kabbalistic texts. His books include: *The First Steps to a New Jewish Spirit, Spiritual Intimacy, Paradigm Shift, From Aging to Sage-ing,* and *Worlds of Jewish Prayer.*

Rev. Jürgen Schwing, M.A., is a board certified chaplain at Kaiser Permanente Medical Center and Hospice in Walnut Creek, California. He studied religion and philosophy at Frankfurt and Heidelberg Universities in Germany and holds an M.A. in Religion and Psychology from the Pacific School of Religion in Berkeley, California. He completed clinical training in spiritual care and counseling at Stanford University Medical Center and California Pacific Medical Center in San Francisco.

Mary Ann Scofield, Ph.D., RSM, holds a Ph.D. in Theology and an M.A. in Spiritual Direction. She is a founding member of Spiritual Directors International. Mary Ann is a Mercy Center staff member; her ministry is primarily spiritual direction, retreat direction, supervision, and the formation of spiritual directors and supervisors.

Huston Smith, Ph.D., was Professor of Philosophy at M.I.T. for fifteen years. Holder of twelve honorary degrees, Smith's fourteen books include *The World's Religions* (which has sold over two million copies), and *Why Religion Matters.* His film documentaries on Hinduism, Tibetan Buddhism, and Sufism have all won international awards.

Jeremy Taylor, D. Min., is an ordained Unitarian Universalist minister, who has worked with dreams for more than thirty years. His books on Jungian-oriented dream work include *The Living Labyrinth, Dreams and the Symbolism of Waking Life, Where People Fly and Water Runs Uphill,* and *Dream Work.* Also, he has taught in the schools and seminaries at the Graduate Theological Union in Berkeley, California, for more than thirty years.

Acknowledgments

The chapters in this book developed from presentations at a conference entitled "The Heart of Spiritual Guidance." The conference was hosted and sponsored by my own institution, the Institute of Transpersonal Psychology. I would like to thank the administration and staff of the Institute for all their help and support with the conference, especially to the ITP William James Center and its director Professor Arthur Hastings for providing initial financial support.

I am very grateful for the tremendous dedication and hard work of Hayden Reynolds who was our conference coordinator. He worked on event preparations for months, and the conference would not have happened without him. Barbara Stefik donated the printing of our conference materials. Paula Yue handled the food. Richard Page recorded the conference. Student volunteers who played critical roles in the preparation and hosting of the conference are Dan Gaylin, Vera Lind, Marie May, Natasha McLennan, Margaret Meriwether, Stelli Munnis, Takanari Tajiri, Valentine Mckay Riddell, and Steven Schmitz.

I would especially like to thank Krista Regedanz who transcribed and edited all the chapters in this book. Her patience, humor, and editing skills were invaluable.

I am deeply grateful for the friendship and support of Roy M. Carlisle, senior editorial consultant. In thirty-five years of writing and publishing, I have never worked with such an intelligent, knowledgeable, enthusiastic, and encouraging editor. Because of Roy's hard work and dedication, this book came together with extraordinary speed and smoothness.

My wife Ayhan Frager and our sons John and Kenan have provided me great support before, during, and after my work on this book. Their love and patience have given me essential nourishment and joy in my life.

A Word About the Book

Recently I heard a sermon at an installation service for a new associate who was joining a church's pastoral team. The message from this well-educated and well-spoken senior pastor highlighted the changing emphases that emerge in parish ministry, seemingly in every decade. Although I would have made a slightly different list for what I thought was the "hot" topic in clergy circles for each decade, we did agree that presently the ministry of "spiritual direction" was the emergent trend in every denomination and among a wide variety of ministerial leaders and clergy. He shared a note of caution about becoming too focused on these changing trends as his way of charging the new associate to stay focused on her unique gifts and calling. I did agree with that charge but not with the caution about shifting emphases. My sense is that these decade- long emerging trends are ways in which the Spirit speaks to the church universal about what is missing in people's lives. They are a needed corrective to the superficiality and spiritual blindness that often afflicts the church in America.

I also disagreed that "spiritual direction" is a fad that will fade away as a new trend emerges. And this desire for a spiritual companion or spiritual director has not faded at all; in fact this need and desire is growing and crossing boundaries in rather dramatic ways. Spiritual direction training programs have increased over the last fifteen years and continue to attract more and more individuals who feel called to this ministry. I have a friend who did a Ph.D. at a well-known evangelical seminary, trained to become a spiritual director with Benedictine monks, and now has a full time practice and ministry as a spiritual director for people from all walks of life. A few years ago that would have been an unusual example, today it is not. Twenty years ago the title "spiritual director" would have been an unfamiliar term for most people except Catholic and Episcopal clergy. Today Evangelicals, Protestants, Jews, Muslims, as well as Catholics, people from all faith paths are training to become spiritual directors and even training at the same places. Again that would have been unusual a few years ago and now it is de rigueur for a program to include persons from diverse faith orientations.

This book has emerged out of that growing and energetic world of spiritual guidance (usually now referred to as spiritual direction) which is simultaneously ancient and new. Fifteen well known and respected experts in the field have shared their own vision of what is vital and important in this world, and where they think we might be headed in the years to come in regards to this ministry.

It takes a Herculean effort to bring together a group of experts of this stature to focus on one task. And it has been my pleasure and privilege to get to know the "force" behind this effort. Robert Frager is a legend in the world of spirituality and psychology for many reasons. Foremost, probably, has been his dedication to establishing a school of now international reputation, the Institute of Transpersonal Psychology in Palo Alto. From this base Robert has written books, taught, lectured, provided guidance and oversight for ITP's growth as an institution, and specifically led ITP's program for spiritual guidance and direction, and then generally given of his enormous intellect and gracious spirit to hundreds of students and faculty for more than three decades. Dr. Frager is a man of boundless energy, charisma, and personal warmth, who has made editing this particular volume one of the delights of my career.

It is clear that this esteemed group of contributors believe, as I do, that we need men and women who are dedicated to broadening and deepening the influence of spiritual direction in every aspect of personal and public life. We are a culture desperately in need of this kind of guidance and wisdom. So I am glad that the team at The

Crossroad Publishing Company has dedicated themselves to publishing books of substance and wisdom for spiritual directors, clergy, and lay leaders who feel called to mediate the Presence of Spirit in a culture cursed with a superficial understanding of all things spiritual and divine.

Of Related Interest

Suzanne Buckley, ed.
SACRED IS THE CALL

Presented by Mercy Center, a leading spiritual direction program in the United States, this handbook addresses questions
asked by every spiritual direction trainer about how to present
key topics in a spiritual direction program. It also provides
wise guidance for individual seekers looking to further their
own spiritual growth.

Contributors include such luminaries as Mary Ann Scofield,
Jim Neafsey, Don Bisson, Jim Keegan SJ, Bill Creed SJ,
Lucy Abbott Tucker, Maria Bowen, Joe Driskill, and Jim
Bowler. Topics include contemplative listening, discernment,
the wisdom of the body, ethics, male and female perspectives, sexuality, prayer, and others. Each contribution features
reflection questions and suggestions for further reading.

SUZANNE BUCKLEY, General Editor, holds a B.S. in Organi-
zational Development and an M.A. in Applied Spirituality.
She currently serves as Manager of Mission Advancement at
Mercy Center in San Francisco.

0-8245-2338-5, paperback

crossroad

Of Related Interest

Karen Kuchan, Ph.D.
VISIO DIVINA
A New Practice of Prayer for Healing and Growth

A remarkable new development in Christian prayer!

Join others today who are finding God's healing, forgiveness, and love through Visio Divina. In *Visio Divina*, meditative and healing prayer is used with a particular image that God reveals for the discovery of hidden wounds and desires. Dr. Kuchan weaves together practical explanations of this new practice, along with stories of people who have used it to overcome shame and anger as they discover divine acceptance and love.

KAREN KUCHAN, Ph.D., is the founder and president of the Incarnation Center for Spiritual Growth and an adjunct professor at Fuller Seminary in Pasadena, California.

0-8245-2317-2, paperback

crossroad

Of Related Interest

Timothy M. Gallagher, O.M.V.
SPIRITUAL CONSOLATION
An Ignatian Guide for the Greater Discernment of Spirits

All of us strive to listen to what God wants for our lives. But how can we assess when feelings, even pleasant ones, are signs that God is calling us in a particular direction?

In *Spiritual Consolation,* Timothy Gallagher, a retreat leader and popular author of *The Examen Prayer* and *The Discernment of Spirits*, introduces us to the teachings of Ignatius of Loyola on this crucial question. Through the use of real-life examples and the Ignatian principles from the Second Rule, Fr. Gallagher shows how all of us, especially those with busy religious lives, can learn to hear and follow God's leading.

This book is both the completion of Dr. Gallagher's esteemed Ignatian trilogy and a provocative work in its own right.

"Timothy Gallagher writes exceptionally clearly and attractively.... His writing is marked by a reverence and love for Ignatius' text, and by a gift for clear exposition. This book is a valuable new contribution to the Ignatian literature, one that I welcome warmly. Read it and learn from it."

— *Philip Endean*

TIMOTHY GALLAGHER holds a doctorate from the Gregorian and has been a retreat leader for over two decades. He lives at St. Clement's Shrine in Boston.

0-8245-2429-2, paperback

crossroad

Of Related Interest

Timothy M. Gallagher, O.M.V.
THE DISCERNMENT OF SPIRITS
An Ignatian Guide for Everyday Living

0-8245-2291-5, paperback

Timothy M. Gallagher, O.M.V.
THE EXAMEN PRAYER
Ignatian Wisdom for Our Lives Today

With a foreword by Fr. George Aschenbrenner

This is the first book to explain the examen prayer, one of
the most popular practices in Christian spirituality. Fr. Timothy Gallagher takes us deep into the prayer, showing that the
prayer Ignatius of Loyola believed to be at the center of the
spiritual life is just as relevant to our lives today.

0-8245-2367-9, paperback

Check your local bookstore for availability.
To order directly from the publisher,
please call 1-800-707-0670 for Customer Service
or visit our Web site at *www.cpcbooks.com.*
For catalog orders, please send your request to the address below.

THE CROSSROAD PUBLISHING COMPANY
16 Penn Plaza, Suite 1550
New York, NY 10001

All prices subject to change.

crossroad